Inkshed Publications

An initiative of the
Canadian Association for the Study of Language and Learning (CASLL)

The publications provide Canadian academics and teachers with an ongoing vehicle to create and maintain dialogue on current scholarship, research, and theory in the domains of language study; composition studies; rhetorical studies; the study of texts and how they are composed, read, and used; the study of literature and response to literature; pedagogy in English studies; language arts and English education; media and communication studies; and related fields. Inkshed Publications is committed to providing a venue for alternative conceptualizations of language and discourse which challenge traditional theories and their attendant pedagogies. Inkshed Publications is also committed to giving voice to emerging, different, and marginalized discourse.

Managing editors of Inkshed Publications:

Laura E. Atkinson, Manitoba Teachers' Society
Pat Sadowy, University of Manitoba
Karen E. Smith, University of Manitoba
Stanley B. Straw, University of Manitoba

Writing in a Community of Practice: Composing Membership in Inkshed

Miriam E. Horne

Winnipeg, Manitoba, Canada

Order this book online at www.trafford.com
or email orders@trafford.com

Most Trafford titles are also available at major online book retailers.

Portions of this book have been taken directly from the dissertation of the author.

Notice for librarians: A cataloguing record for this book is available from
Library and Archives Canada at http://www.collectionscanada.ca/amicus/index-e.html

Printed in the United States of America.

ISBN: 978-1-4669-4192-2 (sc)

Library of Congress Control Number: 2012910079

Trafford rev. 07/03/2012

 www.trafford.com

North America & international
toll-free: 1 888 232 4444 (USA & Canada)
phone: 250 383 6864 ♦ fax: 812 355 4082

Contents

Acknowledgements

This research would not have been possible without the help and support of the Inkshed community. The welcome, the encouragement, and the willingness to participate that I received from community members gave me not just the material to work with, but also the motivation to pursue this research. While I cannot name them all, I owe a particular thank you to Russ Hunt, who willingly answered all my questions, as well as all those who took time to be interviewed, answered questions via email, and shared stories. I am also grateful to Anthony Paré, who not only participated in this research but also provided insight and guidance in understanding and pursuing the themes and stories I gathered.

The patient and careful work of Inkshed Publications, in particular, Pat Sadowy and Karen Smith, has also made the realization of this book possible and I thank them for their vision and perspectives in making this research accessible.

Finally, without the support of and sacrifice of my family, Eric, William, Matthew and Grace, none of this work would have been possible. I thank them for humouring my dinner conversations about CoPs, for asking me questions about what I was doing, and for giving me time to write.

Introduction

The role of writing in building community is an important topic. This book moves us through that process by describing the journey into the fold of a particular writing community. While it may be helpful to describe community membership as a typical journey, it is nonetheless important to interrogate this journey of belonging through examining the specific nature of one such community. Given that both the nature of collaborative writing and community practices are situated, the journey itself is also situated practice. The writing community described in this text is Inkshed, an academic collaborative that has existed over 25 years at the publication of this text.

What is Inkshed? It is the nickname of the Canadian Association for the Study of Language and Learning (CASLL), an organization that has the purpose of exploring relationships among research, theory, and practice in language acquisition and language use, particularly in the Canadian context. Inkshed has a website, listserv, publication group, and annual meetings. The membership is a mixture of mainly

Canadian academics and professional writers from across the provinces and territories. Regional members organize a yearly conference. For these conferences, members are provided with a guiding theme that creates a common thread for member presentations. Following and often during presentations at each one of these conferences, a special type of sharing takes place: members write responses to each of the presentations; they literally *shed ink* on the presentations and then place these response writings on conference tables for others to read and engage in further writing, responses to the responses. Writings in response to the speakers are then gathered together by a team of conference organizers, edited and distributed so that all members, including the presenters, can read the written responses of their community throughout the duration of the conference. As the technology has become available, some responses have been posted online. This writing-in-community response was a forerunner of the current social networks, which became an inevitable consequence of writing collectives online such as wikis, Twitter, online letters to the editor, fan fiction, or Facebook. Inkshedders have always described this conference as a working conference and described the collaborative nature of their responses in writing as a far deeper experience than merely listening to a speaker and/or asking questions at the end of a session. The audience is purposefully engaged. The investment of self is personal.

In this text, Miriam Horne has addressed the nature of this deeper experience. She notes that it is a risk-taking venture and that the feeling of membership goes beyond paying fees to belong. Inkshedders must pay their dues in other ways toward full membership. Legitimate peripheral participation (LPP), as introduced by Jean Lave and Etienne Wenger, is only the beginning. Horne's book provides insight into knowledge about membership and invites us to think about our own and other communities of membership such as school classrooms, Web 2.0, churches, and clubs. We see that peripheral participation is an important and tenuous aspect of membership and that success in this outside margin is important to the nature of how one sees oneself later, on the inside of membership. Horne's interrogation of what it means to become an Inkshedder allows us to interrogate the meaning of membership through collaborative writing, and determine what it really means to become part of a community. The book describes a personal journey into academic writing in community and is a good read for anyone who aspires to that destination.

Karen E. Smith
University of Manitoba

1

Writing and Community: Making Connections

I t's already dark outside on this chilly October day. I watch my classmates struggle in the door wet with the rain that darkens Montreal's skies. I sit at a table near the back of what serves as a dining room during the day. I pretend to be busy reading, hoping that I look more in place than I actually feel. Monday evenings, my first semester as a graduate student in McGill's Faculty of Education, I attend Anthony Paré's course on Writing Across the Curriculum. Fresh out of my undergraduate program I am surrounded by people who are older than me, have been teaching for years, and seem to know exactly why they're here and what they want to do. I, on the other hand, feel like an interloper. As other students join my table, I smile and say hello, but I don't engage any further than that. If I open my mouth too much, the other graduate students might find out how much I don't *know. They might realize that I'm not really good enough to join the academic community.*

After three weeks of this course, I have, I think, perfected my façade. I do the readings for the class well ahead of time. I read each assigned article with a critical eye, finding any weakness, finding whatever the author may have left out, finding the problems. When I arrive in class, as I have this evening, I pretend to be reading something scholarly—something that will make me look smart. When we start our small group discussions, I contribute as little as possible, and limit myself to specific criticisms of the text itself—I don't dare stretch ideas beyond that. In the large class discussions that Anthony brings together for the last part of class, I listen, but I stay silent.

Finally, Anthony arrives, shakes the rain off his jacket, and prepares to get the class started. He has decided that since we're a large class, we will be more comfortable meeting at Thomson House—the graduate student building. We sit in the basement where the restaurant is, and make ourselves comfortable around the large dining room tables. Of course, feeling as insecure as I do as a new graduate student, we could be meeting anywhere and I'd still feel uncomfortable.

"So what I'd like to start with tonight," Anthony begins, "is some writing. Take a few minutes and freewrite about one or both of the articles you read for this evening."

Oh crap. I have to write. I am unsure how to proceed. I am unsure what to say. I worry about writing the right thing, about writing something significant. I take a deep breath, put pen to paper and being to writing, trying, as I go, to sound as articulate and educated as possible.

After a few painful minutes, I finish with what I think are appropriately academic concerns and put my pen down. Too late, I realize that others are still writing. I worry that they have more to say than I do—that once again, I won't measure up. I wonder if I'm going to have to hand this in and hope desperately that Anthony is not actually going to read it. After only a moment of my further fretting, however, Anthony stands and asks for our attention. I find myself silently pleading with him not to ask us to hand them in. I don't know if my ideas are good enough. "Now," says Anthony, "I'd like you to pass your paper two people to your right."

My heart pounds. My stomach churns. I wonder if I have heard correctly. I wonder if he might be crazy.

"Then as you read the text make a line in the margin beside anything that stands out to you, beside anything that resonates with you or you think others would benefit from. Once you've finished, keep passing to the right until you've read all the freewrites at your table."

I feel panic gripping me. I am sure that if other people read this, I will be exposed for the fraud that I am. I kick myself for sitting at the back of the room and wish that I were sitting by the door at the front so I could make an escape to the bathroom.

Despite the strength of my angst, everyone seems to be complying with Anthony's request. The papers are starting to move around the table. I can't help but notice, however, that others look uncomfortable as well. The woman next to me mutters an apology as she hands hers over. Maybe, I think, I'm not the only one who feels uncomfortable. I begin to read.

I finish reading the first paragraph and glance around to see who the author might be. Clearly, she has had far more teaching experience than I have. I realize it's much easier to critique someone who is far away and faceless. I realize that if she is as uncomfortable as I am, then I need to be more sensitive in how I respond. I do as Anthony suggests, and I draw a line in the margin beside her first paragraph. I think there is something of value in here that is interesting to think about—I realize I don't have to come up with a criticism, just think about what she has said.

As I take the next text that is waiting at my elbow, I glance up to see where my text is. Someone across the table is reading it. I note, with relief, that she is not laughing, that she is even drawing a line beside something I have written.

The activity continues. I continue to read, sensitive to those writers who are sitting with me. When my page finally makes its way back to me, I am amazed to see that parts of it have several lines in the margin beside it; I am amazed that someone has valued my input; I am amazed that no one has laughed at me. Perhaps, I muse, there is a place for me in this community after all. As I leave class later that evening, I find myself walking out with two of the women at my table, talking with them, and for the first time, feeling like maybe I do belong.

Belonging, membership—these are powerful concepts that drive and shape human identity. They are wrapped up not just in communities but in individual strengths and insecurities as well. The preceding vignette draws on personal experience to describe and introduce some of the angst and tension that sometimes accompanies joining a new community—more specifically, academia. While the angst and tension may not be a surprise (even if we rarely talk about it overtly), the role that writing had in facilitating membership in academia may be. It was not until after that challenging writing experience described in the opening vignette that I began to feel like I belonged either in that graduate class or in academia at all. What happened that evening that changed how I felt? What part did my insecurities play in participation? What happened that allowed me to be part of the community and not feel so fraudulent? What does it mean to identify with and belong to a community? What was it about writing and the immediacy of sharing that writing that changed my perspective of my classmates and my feelings of fitting in? What is the role of writing in creating/developing a membership in a community?

The questions that this vignette introduces are the same questions that I sought to answer in this book because, while much work has been done that examines community membership and that connects writing to its social setting or community, little attention has been paid to how being able to carry out that writing practice actually facilitates membership in that social setting or community or the sometimes painful human element that accompanies membership. Take, for example, the work of Wenger (1998) who carefully described the ways that groups of people come together through common interests that lead to shared practices to form what he called communities of practice (CoPs). The theory behind CoPs, as I explain in more detail further in this chapter, provides a useful way of understanding how people come together through common practices to form units we call communities. By drawing on the practices in which people engage, Wenger explored functionality, learning and human engagement. However, despite his attention to practice, he did not explicitly address the role of language in general or writing more specifically as a driving practice in forming community (Barton & Hamilton, 2005). Similarly, despite exploring identity and learning within these communities and despite detailed and insightful descriptions of the workplace, Wenger did not explicitly address the human experience of participation or personal angsts, or predispositions that might impact participation.

Genre theorists such as Miller (1984), Freadman (1994), Schryer (1994), Paré (2002) and Artemeva (2006) had different views. For example, Miller (1984), with her notion of genre as "typified rhetorical actions based in recurrent situations" (p. 159), reconceptualized thinking about writing to locate it within its social structures and to recognize the dynamic interconnection between writing and social setting. As a result, we have benefitted from a vast body of research that examines a wide variety of text types and the communities in which they were generated—for example, Schryer (1994) and medicine, Medway (2002) and architecture, and Paré (2002) and social work to name a few. However, while their works make essential contributions to understanding writing practices, there is much less attention to how these practices contribute to the human experience of the process of learning to write within a community or the human cost of participating in a genre. What is the lived significance of carrying out writing tasks? In other words, how do people learn these writing practices and what are the experiences associated with that learning? How does one know if one has learned successfully? What are the consequences on community membership of not mastering the writing practice? Furthermore, how does that affect the individual?

In order to explore the relationship between writing and community membership, I draw on the experience of a five-year ethnographic study in which I examined the writing practices of an academic community that not only studied and researched and taught writing as a socially mediated and contextualized act, but also practiced it as a heuristic and dialogic activity amongst its members. Although I focus on one specific academic community, I believe that much of the experience I describe will resonate with readers who have experiences joining other academic communities. To this end, I have utilized descriptive vignettes (as I did in the opening of this chapter) to recreate some of the human issues less talked about but equally important in joining an academic community. By presenting issues in this way, I draw on notions from qualitative research that recreate situations in the form of stories to broaden perspectives.

Over the course of five years, I not only studied the practices of but also became a member of the Canadian Association for the

Study of Language and Learning (CASLL). This community, which emerged in the early 1980s out of a need for Canadian scholars to connect and work with each other, has filled an important role in Canadian writing studies. For over twenty-five years it hosted annual conferences, and continues to publish a newsletter, host a listserv and publish work important to writing studies. CASLL continues to be a recognized institution in Canadian writing studies. It is currently undergoing change to find the most appropriate ways to meet the needs of its members.

CASLL is known less formally and more commonly as Inkshed. When I refer, in the body of this text, to Inkshed with an "*I*," I am referring to the CASLL community. The community takes this nickname from a writing activity called inkshedding—an activity in which participants respond in writing to a common prompt and then share what they have written with each other, and an activity which, when written with a small "i," refers to the activity, not the community.

Inkshedding, I learned after the fact, was the writing activity that Anthony took us through that October evening in class, the one I described at the beginning of this chapter. As Anthony had us do, participants at annual Inkshed conferences responded to common prompts (conference presentations or sessions rather than the readings we were doing as graduate students), then shared these written responses and underlined, marked-up or otherwise highlighted in others' writings any passages that seemed significant. At conferences, an editorial committee then collected all the responses, selected the sections that had been most highlighted, typed them, copied them, and distributed these thoughts to all participants in order to enhance discussions and ideas. This process happened over and over again during a four-day, annual conference.

From that first evening in which I was introduced to inkshedding and in the subsequent years of becoming an Inkshed member, I observed relationships between writing, community membership and identity. This book draws on my experiences in the Inkshed community to explore the process of community membership and the role that writing has in that process. My journey of membership provides insights into the often overlooked personal process of membership. Despite theories that explicate the experience, there has been little attention to the lived-through experience of both the angst and joy of negotiating human relationships. This book is an attempt to articulate and highlight that experience.

My experience with inkshedding and the Inkshed community embodies two fundamental and interconnected perspectives that help to explicate the experience of learning to inkshed and learning to belong to an academic community and, therefore, to address the role of writing in community membership. First, writing is a social act—an idea that draws on theories of social constructionism and recognizes the importance of social context and human interaction in the production of written texts. Second, communities are shaped and determined by their practices, and in academia, writing is an essential practice. Understanding communities through their practices resonates with theories developed by Lave and Wenger (1991) and Wenger (1998) who described what they called communities of practice (CoPs). These two notions are important because, when understood together, they help to make sense of the experiences and activities that contribute to membership in the various communities in which individuals participate, and, as I will illustrate in this book, these practices shape and form identities.

Writing as a Social Act

When I say that writing is a social act, I align myself with the ideas of scholars such as LeFevre (1987), Berlin (1988), Bizzell (1983), and Dias, Freedman, Medway and Paré (1999). Dias et al. articulated their stance by arguing that:

> The contexts of writing not only influence it (facilitating it or frustrating it or nudging it in a particular direction) but are integral to it. The context is not simply the contingent circumstances within which we happen to switch on the writing motor. Writing is not a module that we bring along and plug into any situation we find ourselves in. Rather, the context constitutes the situation that defines the activity of writing; to write *is* to address the situation by means of textual production. (Dias et al., 1999, p. 17)

Proponents of this position understand that writing is not simply an isolated, multi-step process through which a writer ends up with a structurally, linguistically, and content-appropriate text. Rather, writing is a socially mediated act. It is dependent on specific social and rhetorical situations. No writer works in isolation, but, to write successfully, is subject to the values, attitudes and demands of the context in which she writes. Writing is imbued with connotations that carry forward into social interactions. Understanding the implications of context is important in writing studies as a reminder that writing "is not a discrete clearly definable skill learned once and for all" (Dias et al., 1999, p. 9). Rather, it is "the outcome of continuing collaboration, of interactions that involve other people and other texts" (p. 10).

Thus, when Anthony first guided us through the uncomfortable writing task that I described at the beginning of this book, he was setting up a situation in which the social context was immediately relevant and meaningful. It made a difference whether we wrote or not. The social context—the small group of graduate students responding to the same text—gave us a meaningful context in which to share productive interactions through writing.

This social contextualization of writing finds its foundations in the work of social constructionists. Work by Kuhn (1970), Geertz (1973), and Rorty (1979) laid a foundation for understanding basic social theories of knowledge, community, and language. Social constructionist theorists argue that knowledge is created when experts within communities use common language to describe and draw conclusions about what they see. As the majority of a community agrees on the interpretation of observations, knowledge is created and established. Our small group of graduate students was tapping into the expertise of experts in the field and as a microcommunity went through the process of interpreting and creating understanding together through our writing.

Knowledge, therefore, is a consensual understanding and interpretation of observed phenomena. Established facts change only when enough anomalies occur to challenge established assumptions, and experts are forced to revisit and recreate their knowledge (Kuhn, 1970). However, as the small group of graduate students at my table illustrated, this knowledge does not exist outside the interpretive framework of communities. The strength of communities provides a paradigm in which to make sense of observations. Our background as education students interested in writing provided the initial paradigm for us to understand our readings. Increased exposure to the work of experts (chosen by the professor) continued to shape that paradigm through the semester bringing us into the larger community of writing studies.

The societies to which we belong impact how we understand or interpret what we see (Geertz, 1973). The way that communities and societies understand or interpret observations and turn them into knowledge is through language. As Bruffee (1986) explained, "We use language primarily to join communities we do not yet belong to and to cement membership in communities we already belong to" (p. 784). This positioning of language within communities points to the importance of understanding language as a practice of communities, and understanding communities as driven by practice.

Communities of Practice

It is useful to understand the complexities of writing as a social act by identifying the social setting or the community in which the writing takes place. The term community, however, is problematic in its breadth. To focus my understanding of community I drew on Wenger (1998) and Lave and Wenger (1991) as well as Rogoff and Lave (1984) who, in their theorizing of communities of practice (CoPs), conceptualized communities through the practices that bring them together. As social constructionists, they posited social structures as the means of learning and development. Wenger (1998) explained the basic idea behind CoPs in the following way:

> Being alive as human beings means that we are constantly engaged in the pursuit of enterprises of all kinds, from ensuring our physical survival to seeking the most lofty pleasures. As we define these enterprises and engage in their pursuit together, we

interact with each other and with the world and we
tune our relations with each other and with the world
accordingly. In other words, we learn.

Over time, this collective learning results
in practices that reflect both the pursuit of our
enterprises and the attendant social relations. These
practices are thus the property of a kind of community
created over time by the sustained pursuit of a shared
enterprise. It makes sense, therefore, to call these
kinds of communities *communities of practice* [italics
his]. (p. 45)

CoPs, according to Wenger (2006), "are groups of people who
share a concern or a passion for something they do and learn how
to do it better as they interact regularly." Or, as Barton and Tusting
(2005) explained, "the starting point for the idea of a community of
practice is that people typically come together in groupings to carry
out activities in everyday life, in the workplace, and in education"
(p. 2). Thus, a CoP is not just a collective, but is a group of people who
participate in shared actions for a common purpose.

According to Wenger, everyone participates in a variety of CoPs
from workplace, to social life, to living situation, to hobby groups.
Co-workers in an office practice a framework of rules, routines, and
rituals. There may be conflict; there may be agreement; there may be
both. Different workers have different responsibilities, and yet, all are
bound together within the same framework that pulls them together.
That is, despite possible conflicts, disparities, and differences,
members of a CoP share an interdependence.

Similarly, students in a study group follow certain patterns and
behaviours in an effort to achieve a collective purpose (e.g., to do well

in class). The study group establishes its own informal characteristics and rules that govern practices of membership (such as how much time is acceptable for chatting, who is responsible for which assignments, and how long meetings will go on). As students meet together they learn together. The learning process incorporates far more than covering the material assigned by the professor. It includes negotiating understandings and meanings together.

Some communities are more tightly structured than others and are easier to identify—like a workplace. Others may be less tangible—like an on-line gaming community the members of which never actually meet face to face, know real names or other characteristics, but who share common interests, purposes, and activities. Often, memberships in communities are left undefined because of the loose nature of the collective.

Because humans tend to be social by nature, memberships in communities are multiple. One might be both a co-worker and part of a student study group. In my case, exploring communities in the background work for this book, I was a student, a researcher, a teacher, a mother, a girlfriend, and a Mormon. Each of these titles represents a different community to which I belonged. Sometimes they overlapped and enhanced each other—like student, researcher and teacher. Other times, however, they came into conflict. I anticipated, for example, that my Mormon community would remain far removed from my academic communities. I was unprepared for and surprised by the ways these communities intersected. In any case, such titles describe a variety of complex social practices in which people engage when they share a common purpose. Within these communities, learning takes place as members participate in practices. As individuals learn to participate in collectives, and feel like they belong to the community, their identities grow to reflect membership in the collective.

Identity

From work in psychology (Bruner, 1990; Tajfel & Turner, 1986) to work in cultural and race studies (Giroux & McLaren, 1994; West, 1993), to literacy studies (Lankshear, Gee, Knobel & Searle, 1997; Street, 1985) and beyond, discussions of identity infuse multiple conversations. I recognize the broad and multi-layered concepts associated with each of the different conversations about identity. I recognize also that identities are complex and dynamic. They consist of a variety of roles that evolve as a result of practices specific to the community. For example, by meeting with students, going to class, and otherwise engaging in teacherly practices, I take on the role of professor. Practices and their subsequent roles vary according to circumstance, that is, according to which collective the individual is most actively taking part in at a given time. Different roles and participation in different communities may conflict or complement each other. As Handley, Sturdy, Fincham and Clark (2006) explained, "individuals bring to a community a personal history of involvement with workplace, social and familial groups whose norms may complement or conflict with one another" (p. 642). Although I am at once mother and teacher, I am more mother when I am at home and engaging in the practices of motherhood. While this often conflicts with my work role as I try to incorporate grading papers and class preparations between meals, laundry and other domestic chores, I continue to maintain membership in both a professional CoP and familial CoP.

This book explores the relationship between writing practices and community. More specifically, it examines how learning to inkshed facilitated an Inkshed identity as a way of understanding writing and membership. Therefore, my purpose is not to get into what constitutes identity per se, but rather, to explore identity as a continuing process of membership.

This view of identity as a process of membership is supported by Wenger (1998), who explained the concept of identity as "a way of talking about how learning changes who we are and creates personal histories of becoming in the context of our communities" (p. 5). In other words, identity is about how individuals change and are reshaped as they learn to participate in collectives. Thus, in my study I sought to explore an experience of "becoming" in the Inkshed community.

Like Wenger (1998), who posited that identity is co-constituted with communities and their practices, I believe that "Our identity includes our ability and our inability to shape the meanings that define our communities and our forms of belonging . . . . Building an identity consists of negotiating the meanings of our experience of membership in social communities" (p. 145). In this way identity grows and develops in conjunction with social interactions. Identity and membership are, for my purposes, synonymous. I learned to participate in the Inkshed collective by engaging in community practices. Talking about my membership in the Inkshed community is talking about how I functioned and interacted within that community based on my constantly evolving identity.

This perspective, that identity depends on social interactions, draws on a Bakhtinian understanding of identity, one that sees identity as being co-constituted through dialogue with others. Taylor (1994), who used the work of Bakhtin in his philosophical pursuit of a dialogic self, explained that individuals develop identity, or learn to participate in a community, through interactions with others. He said, "We define our identity always in dialogue with, sometimes in struggle against, the things our significant others want to see in us" (p. 32). Thus, "becoming in the context of the community" (Wenger, 1998, p. 5), or changing who one is, happens through meaningful interaction with others in the collective. In Inkshed, an individual's identity or membership may change; one may learn to engage in the community through meaningful exchange of language with others.

The social interactions in which individuals engage help to shape and form identities. Identity is a developing process of membership. In the study of Inkshed, part of my goal was to look at the process of arriving with my personal histories, roles, and practices (e.g., mother, teacher, and student), and to explore the experience of learning how to fully participate in Inkshed. In other words, this study looks at the process of becoming an Inkshedder. Becoming an Inkshedder happens through a process of learning to participate. That actual learning process can be explicated by the notion of legitimate peripheral participation (LPP).

Legitimate Peripheral Participation

Communities of practice are situations in which learning takes place. The community's practices facilitate that learning. Legitimate peripheral participation, as described by Lave and Wenger (1991), is an often overlooked part of the process of learning in communities. In this section I give a brief overview of LPP and its relevance to this study of the Inkshed community and the inkshedding writing activity. I begin this overview with the words of Lave and Wenger (1991):

> Learners inevitably participate in communities of practitioners and . . . the mastery of knowledge and skill requires newcomers to move toward full participation in the sociocultural practices of a community. Legitimate peripheral participation provides a way to speak about the relations between newcomers and old-timers, and about activities, identities, artifacts, and communities of knowledge and practice. It concerns the process

by which newcomers become part of a community of practice. (p. 29)

Essentially, LPP describes a process in which learning takes place through social practices. Learning, Lave and Wenger argued, is not a process of isolated bits of knowledge being planted in the head of a student to be applied later in a test situation. Instead, learning is the process of acquiring skills by doing or by participating in meaningful ways in a community of practice, or in Wenger's (1998) words, LPP is the "process by which newcomers become included in a community of practice" (p. 100).

In order for newcomers to a community to participate in that community, there must be a means by which the newcomer can gain access to the community. In LPP participatory access comes through what Lave and Wenger (1991) identified as peripherality and legitimacy (p. 101).

i. Peripherality

The term peripherality refers to positions that newcomers take in a community. Significantly, the term peripheral in this case does not mean marginal or unimportant. Instead, it describes a position in which one can learn and gain access to the collective. While an old-timer (a term used by Lave and Wenger to describe those members of the community who have had long-term meaningful participation in the community) participates in the community with full responsibility, a newcomer participates, but with less risk or responsibility than an old-timer. Sometimes a mentor facilitates this participation to make the learning process clearer or more manageable. Newcomers are not on the outside looking in at the practice, but are within the practice in a peripheral way. For example,

Lave and Wenger (1991) noted how apprentice tailors "first learn to make hats and drawers, informal and intimate garments for children. They move on to more external, formal garments ending with the Higher Heights suits" (p. 71). This example shows how apprentices move from tasks where the risk or cost of failure is low to a position in which they have learned all the practices required for the highest level of sewing. Through careful and patient engagement, new tailors learn the practices that move them to a position of expertise or full participation within the community.

This initial peripheral participation is also evident in the Inkshed community. Chapter 2 details the frequent feelings of anxiety that accompany a peripheral position in Inkshed and elaborates on the impacts of this positioning on membership in the community. In fact, this entire project in Inkshed was an exploration of this peripheral positioning and the movement that takes place through participation to finding a location of full membership in the collective.

ii. Legitimacy

The other essential aspect to gaining access to a community is having legitimate participation. Every newcomer needs to be "treated as a potential member" (Wenger, 1998, p. 101). Legitimacy describes the quality of the participation. Tasks and responsibilities are real and genuine, and contribute in a meaningful way to the collective (although for a newcomer, not so much as to jeopardize the community). Without the genuine potential to join the community, the newcomer will never be able to move from the periphery to full participation. As Wenger (1998) explained:

> Granting the newcomers legitimacy is important because they are likely to come short of what the

community regards as competent engagement. Only with enough legitimacy can all their inevitable stumblings and violations become opportunities for learning rather than cause for dismissal, neglect, or exclusion. (p. 101)

In other words, legitimacy opens a doorway to meaningful participation. This issue comes into play later in my discussion of how texts are circulated and read. I explore the ways in which my participation was legitimized and the impact this had on my own participation.

This book is an exploration of inkshedding as a social act. I look at inkshedding not only as a social writing practice, but as a practice that builds community. As well, this book tells the story of how learning to inkshed created an Inkshed identity for me. While I focus on my experiences in CASLL, I believe there is much that will resonate with readers as they reflect on their own experiences of joining academic communities. For those not familiar with Inkshed, Appendix A includes a brief historical overview of the community, followed in Appendix B by a list of the locations of each of the community's annual conferences. As the opening vignette implies, the research that has gone into this book is qualitative in nature. I have included a detailed explanation of methodologies in Appendix C.

In order to explore the experience of membership in a logical and meaningful way, I begin by first exploring what constitutes an Inkshed identity, in other words, what constitutes membership for full participants in the community. I then structure the remaining chapters around the different steps of inkshedding and use each step as an image for a larger human experience and as a step toward participation in the collective. In Chapter 2 I draw on personal experiences, experiences of self-proclaimed Inkshedders, and the development of the community itself to come to an understanding of the practices (specifically writing) and values that reinforce each other to form Inkshed. In Chapter 3 I look at the initial stage of inkshedding—writing the text. I describe this stage in detail, but also look at the challenges that this stage presents to newcomers seeking membership. I look at the vulnerability that emerges as a powerful theme in Inkshedders' stories and the ways that newcomers deal with this reaction both to public writing and to being newcomers to a community.

In the second stage of inkshedding, texts are circulated, read and highlighted. In Chapter 4 I look at issues of democracy at this stage a well as the influence that highlighting can have on identity and membership. In this chapter I explore not only paper texts and the way they are marked, but I also make a case for looking at conference participants themselves as texts who are circulated, read, and marked. The ways that the collective responds to both paper and human texts impacts the ways in which newcomers are able to participate in the collective. That is, interactions influence membership.

In Chapter 5 I look at the final two stages of inkshedding in which highlighted texts are excerpted, typed, copied and redistributed for further discussion. Looking at this stage as publication, I explore experiences of being public. I also look at this stage of inkshedding as a microcosm for the kinds of publication experiences that take place in academia. I show how publication is an essential component of community membership in academia.

Finally, in Chapter 6, I recap the contributions that this research makes both to theories of writing as socially situated and to theories of CoPs. I also discuss the concept of identity and look at two of the broader implications to which these discussions point.

In short, these chapters work together to explore the experience of becoming an Inkshedder and the role that inkshedding had in that process. By examining a community that values writing as dialogic interaction, this study magnifies the role that writing has in community membership. The process of inkshedding and the process of learning to belong weave and grow together in mutually dependent ways.

2

Identity: Parts That Make the Whole

I t's Mother's Day. I just skipped out on the Inkshed AGM that comes at the end of the conference with the excuse that I'd like to be able to get home and have some time with my kids while it's still Mother's Day. They are not impressed that they didn't get to make me breakfast in bed (why they think they can only do it on this particular Sunday once a year, I'm not quite sure). But the promise of homemade cards and tissue paper flowers is not the real reason I left. No, I'm completely overwhelmed. I need time alone with my thoughts. And so I whisk down highway 401 heading for home trying to figure out what has just happened to me.

Last night was the talent show. Most of the time I was roaring with laughter with everyone else. Red Green teaches writing, a poem about a parrot in class, even a gymnastics routine—who knew academics could be so much fun? But then Susan Drain got up and did a recitation about war. Then she began to sing and by the end of *her number had us all holding hands and singing anti-war songs. It wasn't just that I happen to strongly agree with the anti-war sentiment, or that she has a great voice—no, it was those things combined with something (what, I'm not sure) to induce one of those indescribable moments of transcendence, connection, and profound spirituality that I've had so strongly only a handful of times in my life. I think the last time I felt this profound kind of connection to the universe that rocks my perspective of the world was on my study-abroad trip to Israel when Madison Sowell shared some personal life experiences with us. I was so moved by the experience that I felt utterly speechless for the rest of the afternoon—to the point that Dr. Sowell, I think, was concerned and hung back to ask me how I was doing. But there it is, that's the problem that I'm wrestling with now—not that I've had this powerful experience (I wish I had words to better describe it, but it's one of those feelings that transcends the limits of language)—but where I've had it.*

Any time I've had this feeling before, it's always been somehow church-related—even the intense musical experiences that share the power of reaching into my most intimate inner self have been with other Mormons. How is it possible that I could have, for lack of a better descriptor, a spiritual experience at an academic conference where most of the participants, if not exactly drunk, were at least well lubricated (a big taboo in my Mormon culture.) And yet, here it is, that feeling, that sense of meaning and purpose and connection, and not a Mormon in sight.

When I get home my kids shower me with hugs and kisses and complaints and their arguments. I am drawn back to the present, the here and now. But in the back of my head simmer questions for my foundations. A month later my friend from my days as a Mormon missionary calls. We have been through a lot together and so, when

she asks what's new, I try to describe a little of my experience. "Pum,"
she exclaims using her favorite nickname for me, "you've found your
people!" Yes, I reflect, so I have.

The experiences I describe in this vignette illustrate the feelings
of connection that I had to the Inkshed community and the sense of
membership that I took away from that first conference I attended. This
vignette helps to frame the focus of this chapter with the assumption
that membership in the Inkshed community meant more than being a
dues-paying conference attendee. As my experience suggests, people
who identified with the community and called themselves Inkshedders
had a personal commitment that went beyond professional connections.
In the rest of this chapter I describe major values and practices that
helped to shape membership in the Inkshed collective.

My intent in this book is to describe the experience of taking
on an Inkshed identity—to explore how, through writing practices,
individuals join a community. As I explained previously, I see
membership as a process; however, as Wenger (1998) explained, this
means far more than simply being on a membership list. He argued
that identity is connected to practice and explained that "developing
a practice requires the formation of a community whose members
can engage with one another and thus acknowledge each other as
participants" (p. 175). Thus "practice entails the negotiation of ways
of being a person in what context" (p. 176). In the same way that a CoP
is formed by negotiating identities through practices, so a newcomer
to a CoP that is already formed must negotiate an identity. In this
chapter I attempt to describe what an Inkshed identity is and in the
following chapters I look at inkshedding as a tool for becoming a full
participant in the community and taking on an Inkshed identity.

Any Inkshedder would be hard pressed to come up with a description or explanation of the Inkshed identity that everyone agrees on, and yet there seem to be some inherent commonalities that I point to here. While I am aware that, like any human collective, there are aspects of the community that are uncomfortable, exclusive, difficult to negotiate, and at times, even painful, I do not address those darker issues in this chapter. Some of these are discussed elsewhere. For example, in the following chapter, I discuss discomfort, vulnerability and exposure, and some of the challenging negotiations that take place. Later I look at some of the more exclusive social dynamics that exist. For the purposes of this chapter, however, I draw on my experiences and on the narratives of community members to create a kind of composite image describing the things that make the Inkshed community function. As a result, I discuss many of the positive aspects of Inkshed. Unfortunately, this runs the danger of sounding utopian. I do not mean to limit the darker side of the exploration, however, but leave it for later chapters. In the following pages I explore what it means to be called an Inkshedder. Much of this identity involves writing but is not limited to it. Rather, writing practices, as illustrated in the examples I provide, help to describe this identity. I explore a variety of texts including newsletters, inksheds, the listserv, journals and more to pursue three lines of inquiry, which help to explore what it means to be an Inkshedder. I have categorized them as shared interests, reinforcing values, and collective practices or reification of values.

Shared Interests

While Wenger (1998) argued that communities are not homogenous and that engagement comes through diversity, Inkshedders seemed to share some fundamental similarities. People who attended Inkshed conferences did so because they were interested in writing, particularly the teaching of writing in Canada. While people from other countries have attended the conference, my research shows that the teaching of writing in Canada was an important theme in Inkshed.

Individuals who became Inkshedders shared not only an academic interest in socially situated writing in Canada, but also an interest in collaboration and friendship. This section explores the interest in teaching and facilitating language in a Canadian context, and the value of collaboration and friendships (including the roles of both trust and humour).

It should be noted that while these characteristics appear to be commonalities that draw the collective together, I am not implying the converse. That is, I am not suggesting that everyone who had an interest in socially situated explorations of writing, collaboration and friendship was an Inkshedder. Nor did Inkshedders have a monopoly on these characteristics; in fact, there are many scholars who share these characteristics but do not share in the Inkshed community. These are, rather, descriptions of shared characteristics that worked together in this context to facilitate the functioning of the collective and the means through which individuals were, in a community of practice, able to mutually engage.

When asked to explain what it meant to be an Inkshedder, self-proclaimed devotee and proselytizer of inkshedding Betsy Sargent responded:

> I guess I'd define the inkshed community as being pretty huge—it would include for me everyone who had ever attended an Inkshed conference or paid dues to receive the newsletter, everyone who had ever been on the listserv, and then every student of anyone

in those preceding categories who had incorporated inkshedding into their teaching practices. And we should probably include as well people who don't use the term "inkshed" but who practice public, focused freewriting as a form of writing-to-learn or exploratory writing in their teaching (. . . as long as the students know ahead of time that the writing isn't going to be private). Once you include that last group, you probably have to include almost everyone who has gone through the National Writing Project in the states and all of their students . . . . [ellipsis hers] (CASLL Listserv, 12/17/2006)

As Betsy admitted, this description is huge, and I am not entirely sure that I feel a connection with every student who has ever been through the National Writing Project the way I did at the talent night I described (nor they with me). However, Betsy's description does raise some interesting perspectives that reflect at least one of the shared interests or commonalities that brought people to Inkshed—beyond the dues and listserv. Implicit in her description is the importance of teaching—not just any teaching, but the teaching of writing, or how to use language. This concern with teaching typifies a common interest of those who described themselves as Inkshedders.

Teaching and Language

While organizations like the Canadian Association for the Study of Discourse and Writing (CASDW) (formerly known as CATTW—Canadian Association of Teachers of Technical Writing) or the Canadian Society for the Study of Rhetoric (CSSR) tend to focus on scholarship and research, my experiences suggest that Inkshed seemed to have a fundamental concern with teaching, with facilitating learning, and with helping students to use language in socially meaningful ways (i.e., to produce language expecting a real and meaningful response). As Anthony Paré observed: "Inkshedding was made to 'free' the student—to find a voice in the academic context (Personal interview, 2/1/2007).

The original notion of the inkshedding practice was inspired by a desire to help students. This concern also helped to shape the community. Many original Inkshedders share this conviction. For example, in an open-ended focus group discussion, Rick Coe explained what he felt people who came to the conference had in common: "I think somebody once identified it as caring about students, and caring about teaching—in relation to language (Focus group interview, 5/13/2005).

This comment provoked a similar point of view from veteran Inkshedders Doug Vipond, Russ Hunt and Nan Johnson who pointed out that people who participated in Inkshed did so because they chose to focus on teaching and language. They were not there by accident:

> Doug: It's self-selected, partly. People are opting in or opting out.
> Nan: And what's the means by which one does that selection? It is, we care about students and we care about teaching, yes—
> Russ: And we care about language—
> Nan: We come and spend four days and we talk about pedagogy and writing, and these ideas, right, for four days. And there's a certain self-selection I think. (Focus group interview, 5/13/2005)

Thus, those who came to Inkshed conferences and participated in other Inkshed activities did so because they chose to pursue the study of language and learning by focusing on facilitating students. Those who did not share this focus as a primary concern found other communities to facilitate their scholarly work. As Roger Graves explained in identifying the various roles of the major academic communities concerned with writing in Canada:

> CATTW [now CASDW] offers an alternative identity, and for people specifically in technical/professional writing, that name may have a greater claim on them. Some belong to CSSR, and the new writing centre group [the Canadian Writing Centres Association, CWCA] offers a greater recognition for those who work that end of the field. (CASLL Listserv, 12/13/2006)

While not everyone who feels or has felt passionately about academic writing instruction in Canada has been an Inkshedder, those who call themselves Inkshedders care deeply about the study and teaching of writing.

Language and Teaching in Canada

People who participated in Inkshed conferences as community members were not only concerned with teaching and language in general, but had a special interest in this role in Canada.

Inkshed was born out of a need for a forum to discuss writing studies in Canada. In the first newsletter, Jim Reither (1982a) emphasized the Canadian focus he hoped the newsletter would have. He explained that:

This newsletter is offered to all educators in Canada interested in the processes and pedagogies of writing and reading. As a forum whose primary objective is to intensify the relationship between theory and practice, it will serve both informative and polemical functions. (p. 1)

This national objective was reinforced in a retrospective session at the 20th annual conference. At the beginning of a posted timeline of Inkshed history, the writer of one comment asserted: "Inkshed starts with the assumption that there is a Canadian context for writing instruction" (The Wall, Inkshed XX, 2003).

Thus, although Americans attended the conference, there was definitely a Canadian focus to it. The value of this Canadian focus has been articulated by several Inkshedders. Doug Brent observed:

I think what holds Inkshed together as a community is a common interest in language and learning from a Canadian perspective plus the indy [i.e., independent] feel of a conference not connected to a big gathering (e.g., CATTW and the Congress [Congress of the Humanities and Social Sciences]). (CASLL Listserv, 12/15/2006)

Being able to talk about teaching and writing in a specifically Canadian setting facilitated the functioning of Inkshed as a community. Stan Straw echoed this sentiment as he explained that even though Inkshedders were a diverse group of individuals from a variety of backgrounds, the Canadian nature of the community pulled the collective together and set it apart from others. He wrote:

Inkshed is unique in that it invites English department people, writing center people, writing program people, even people from business and government, and *people from education* [emphasis his] to be a part if they choose. It is partly this cross-fertilization that makes Inkshed a community unlike others. Although CCCCs [Conference on College Composition and Communication] has an implicit invitation to educationalists (though we are all educationalists), I think Inkshed is more explicit (and smaller and Canadian—both good things). The name of the organization (Canadian Association for the Study of Language and *Learning* [emphasis his]—notice it's language, not writing) seems to me to capture the group because we are all interested in how are [sic] people learn and use language. (CASLL Listserv, 12/14/2006)

Part of this emphasis on Canadianism has been realized through publications supported by Inkshed. For example, Inkshed XXIII started with a book launch celebrating the work done by Roger and Heather Graves in *Writing Centres, Writing Seminars, Writing Culture: Writing Instruction in Anglo-Canadian Universities*. As the title suggests, this book looked at the way writing programs have developed in post-secondary institutions across Canada. The result of the book launch at the conference (whose theme was "Context is Everything: Everything is Context") was a highlighting throughout the weekend of the distinctions between Canadian writing programs (and the Canadian approach to writing in general) and the work going on in the United States (Field notes, 5/7/2006).

The way that this focus on being Canadian may have been important to the Inkshed collective is that by creating an "other" (i.e., American counterparts), Inkshed reinforced the "we." As part of an online discussion about the nature of the Inkshed community with deep and careful responses such as Stan Straw's above, Brock MacDonald responded with an apparently whimsical observation about the discussion. He wrote:

> One thing strikes me: how very Canadian this is! Are we a community? (Are we a nation?) Are we losing our identity? What IS our identity?—etc, etc, etc. I suppose if we didn't fret over these things from time to time, being Canadians, that would be a sign that our community WAS in trouble . . . . [ellipsis his] (CASLL Listserv, 12/14/2006)

Brock's observation is more significant than he may have intended. While some Americans do attend the conference, there is a definite recognition that writing studies in Canada is slightly different from writing studies in the United States, and Inkshed provides a forum to discuss writing specifically in Canada. This seems to resonate with the birth of Inkshed and the need to address or, at the very least, explore differences between writing studies in Canada and the United States—an emphasis that Canadian needs are not the same as American.

An important part of writing studies and pedagogy in Canada (and the driving force behind the creation of the *Inkshed* newsletter) is the opportunity to collaborate, network, and draw from resources of other Canadian practitioners. Thus, another common interest that Inkshedders shared was the desire for interaction with others who shared their teaching interests—whether, as Straw indicated, they came from English departments or government offices.

Networking and Friendship

When people share common interests, it is natural that they develop acquaintances and friendships. Wenger (1998) explained that through participation and mutual engagement, mutual relationships arise. He described how relationships may evolve in communities of practice (CoPs) by explaining:

> When it [mutual engagement] is sustained, it connects participants in ways that can become deeper than more abstract similarities in terms of personal features or social categories. In this sense, a community of practice can become a very tight node of interpersonal relationships. (p. 76)

Thus, according to Wenger, relationships in CoPs work on a functional level to further the realization of the community goals, practices and responsibilities, but may also become more personal and deep. Inkshed conferences encouraged both of these kinds of relationships. In the same way that all professional conferences and organizations facilitate networking, the exchange of ideas, and collaboration between peers, Inkshed also recognized and valued professional networking, advice, and other forms of peer support. Explaining her reason for being part of Inkshed, one participant wrote: "I value the possibility for professional networking" (Inkshedding text, 5/9/2004). Networking, however, is not limited to knowing the field and what is going on, it also means turning to colleagues for professional support. As Roger Graves explained: "In some sense it [being part of the Inkshed community] means knowing people or knowing of people; another sense is feeling that you could email or even phone one of those people, which I have done" (CASLL Listserv, 12/13/2006).

In other words, it is important to know people in the field, but Inkshed also provided an opportunity to draw on others' backgrounds, experiences, and expertise. Even now, when the community is undergoing a redefinition, Inkshedders both expect to be and appreciate being resources for their colleagues. This kind of collaboration has been encouraged since the inception of the newsletter in the early 1980s. In the first few months of its existence, Jim Reither (1982b) sought to establish lists of experts in various aspects of reading and writing that other people could draw on for assistance. He wrote:

> As an initial project for this Newsletter, I am compiling a list of educators in Canada who are sufficiently expert in matters of theory or practice that they can offer their services as consultants. If you have that kind of expertise, please send me your name, address, and a list of topics (the more precisely defined the better) on which you are sufficiently expert to act as a consultant. Alternatively, recommend someone else, providing me with the same information. (p. 7)

The conscientious effort to draw on expertise in the community continued to grow over the years. While it began with Jim Reither's call for volunteers (in the days before the popularity of email), it later moved from a list of experts in specific areas to a state where members volunteered their expertise on demand. Some of this volunteering was evident in discussions on the listserv. There Inkshedders across Canada happily offered their insights into such matters as the difference between writing instruction in the United States and Canada, plagiarism, and writing centres in Canada (including their history, development, use, and operation). Sometimes the group focused on very specific issues: one lengthy discussion centred on National Cliché Day. My own research was greatly facilitated by this electronic networking. I was able to reach an audience of Inkshedders at once to ask questions, clarify ideas, and gain input into my research.

As my earlier quote from Wenger explained, however, relationships in CoPs can become deeply interpersonal. Relationships in Inkshed illustrate the ways in which they may go beyond professional collaboration and networking. They extend to personal support and friendship. For example, when colleague Natasha Artemeva received the Outstanding Dissertation Award in Technical Communication from the Conference on College Composition and Communication (CCCC), Anthony Paré sent out an announcement on the listserv to this effect celebrating her success. Responses flooded the listserv. The responses that were sent to Natasha via the CASLL listserv were not only about professional support, but also good will and friendship. These kinds of relationships were common in Inkshed. Another example can be seen in the unlikely case of vacation plans. One summer, when driving from Montreal to Cape Breton, I needed a halfway point to spend the night with my family. Learning of this in a side note to a different conversation, Russ Hunt invited us to stay with him. We did so and he and his wife Anne spent many hours entertaining and hosting my three young children and me. The kids still tell "remember when" stories of our day at their home and wonder when we can visit again.

Friendships like this emerged between Inkshedders because they care about their work and they care about each other. As one person explained when describing her introduction to Inkshed:

> I found people who talked my language, though they often disagreed with my—and others'—words. They were passionate about the word, utterly non-stuffy, took risks, wanted to find out rather than score points, and knew how to laugh and play. (Inkshedding text, 5/9/2004)

This writer described a high level of commitment to the teaching and study of writing (they were passionate about the "word"), but juxtaposed this with an image of fun through "laugh and play." Thus she described how she was able to establish relationships in the community, both professionally and socially.

Tania Smith explained this phenomenon in a slightly different way, but explicitly pointed not just to opportunities to network, but also to build friendships. She wrote:

> I go to Inkshed and participate in its listserv for the sense of community and unity of a single-session conference (no concurrent sessions) where you get to know new people and reconnect with old friends, and of course for the practical advice and ideas that accompany the deep insights and theories. (CASLL Listserv, 12/13/2006)

As these two examples illustrate, friendship in Inkshed was highly valued and this shaped the nature of interactions and the way the community emerged. As one person explained:

> At one time about 10 years ago or so, we old-timers started getting messages that Inkshed was getting to be a sort of club of old friends and new people were having trouble breaking in. This may have been a phase of cultural growth—we were not aware of shutting anyone out, but we really were a bunch of old friends and tended to run into corners and catch up on what had happened in our lives. (Inkshedding text, 5/9/2004)

As this excerpt suggests, conferences (primarily) facilitated friendships and these were important for Inkshed participants. Even though these friendships may have made some newcomers uncomfortable, they kept others coming back. The importance of these friendships is reflected in comments like "Inkshed is my family" (Personal conversations with long-time Inkshedders, 5/8/2004; 5/6/2006). For people who made this comparison, Inkshed filled a role of supporter, nurturer, and caregiver by giving individuals a safe and encouraging place to belong. Thus, as my opening vignette described, relationships in Inkshed extended beyond professional networking and collaboration. Rather, they were and continue to be profound, personal, and strong relationships. These relationships helped to form the kind of identity that Wenger (1998) described when he explained that "building an identity consists of negotiating the meanings of our experience of membership in social communities" (p. 145). Developing relationships with community members facilitates identification with those members and therefore with the community. As Inkshedders developed relationships with each other in an Inkshed context, they strengthened an Inkshed identity, or membership in the Inkshed community.

Trust

One of the things that emerged from these deeper, more caring and personal relationships was a sense of trust. Trust typifies another value that those who call themselves Inkshedders shared—a sense of safety. Through a collegial setting, Inkshedders encouraged risk taking. This happened in the inkshedding activity itself in which participants were encouraged to share new or edgy thinking, but also at all levels of interaction. For example, one reminiscence in a 20th anniversary retrospective said simply of one conference, "There was a hot tub." This simple statement is loaded with meaning. Sitting in a close, intimate space clad in minimal clothing suggests a setting in which trust is essential—trust that no one will laugh at you in your bathing suit, trust that you will expose yourselves together.

Risk taking was also encouraged in presentation formats. Traditional talking head presentations were more the exception than the rule. The call for papers typically included guidelines inviting nontraditional formats. For example, in the call for papers for the 2007 conference (Graves, Hyland & Graves, 2006) the conference organizers explained:

> Inkshed has always been a "working" conference that encourages alternative, if not completely transgressive, presentations. We encourage group presentations; demonstrations; activities; and imaginative or creative readings. Participants are strongly encouraged to

> "Inkshed" or respond in writing to presentations and
> to share these responses. (p. 17)

In the years I attended the conference, I saw plays, skits, role-plays, videos, and problem solving exercises. People were able to do these non-traditional kinds of presentations because the sense of trust allowed them to try out new ideas. The result was that people felt more comfortable taking risks. Describing this phenomenon, an original Inkshedder wrote: "It's being free to be wrong, take the risk of saying something stupid, just plain taking the risk. It's not a risk I feel comfortable to take in other contexts, other large groups of people" (Inkshedding text, 5/9/2004).

In the Inkshed context, this individual trusted her colleagues and knew that she would still be accepted as part of the collective regardless of mistakes she might make. Roger Graves echoed the importance of this when he expressed that: "It all depends on the sense of vulnerability and whether you feel you're going to be treated right. And I think you have to make it that" (Focus group interview, 5/13/2005).

While exceptions and examples of not being treated right did exist, for the most part Inkshedders made a conscientious effort to be supportive. Their trust and effort at friendship also facilitated this research so that in focus group interviews participants felt free to interact with and respond to each other. Additionally, people were willing to share personal (if not always positive) narratives with me.

In summary, the passion for teaching and writing in a Canadian context, and the passion for collegial interaction that moves into the sphere of friendship, trust and fun, characterize shared interests of those who participated in Inkshed conferences. This group has been purposeful in its drive to facilitate the teaching of reading and writing in Canadian settings and to do so in a collaborative manner. In the following section, I look at the ways these common interests are facilitated through social writing practices.

Reinforcing Values

The relationship between community values and practices is not one way. Practices serve to reinforce community values. In this next section, I briefly introduce some of the practices that reinforce the valuing of teaching and language, and networking and friendship in a Canadian context. I do not go into great detail describing these practices in this section because the following chapters describe the importance of these practices in gaining membership. I do, however, briefly explain the newsletter, the listserv, the format of the conference, and the ways that these reinforce the values of the collective.

Newsletter and Listserv

The Inkshed community values teaching and language (writing and reading) in a Canadian context. It also values networking and friendships. One of the main ways these values are both sustained and reinforced is first, through the newsletter, and, more recently, through the listserv. As explained earlier in this chapter, the explicit purpose of creating the newsletter was to provide a forum in which to discuss issues connected to writing and reading in a Canadian context. The newsletter did this through its content. For example, "provincial reports" noted teaching and research being done at different universities across Canada. These reports included a range of information about writing from a description of writing courses being offered at the University of Alberta as well as the research projects in writing being undertaken by graduate students (Bullock, 1982) to

Rick Coe's (1983) description of the development of writing curricula in schools in British Columbia. The newsletter also included such items as reviews of scholarly articles, conference reports/reviews, and personal reflections, all of which focused on some aspect of teaching and/or studying writing and reading in Canada. As Jim Reither (1983) summarized as he started the second year of the newsletter:

> W&R/T&P has made some modest progress toward achieving one of its objectives—helping to build a sense of community among those of us working in a Canadian academic environment who are interested in writing and reading theory and practice.
>
> But we accomplished more than that, too. W&R/T&P published some nice little articles, notices, and reviews. Some examples: Russ Hunt's "Two Energizing Articles" and "Litmanship Through the Ages: Stephen Potter as Literary Historian"; Chris Bullock's, Rick Coe's, and Murray Evans' "News from the Provinces" reports; Andrea Lunsford's review of several inexpensive journals and two bargain conferences; Anthony Paré's commentary on the need for accountability in the writing courses we teach, and his review of Linda Flower's *Problem-Solving Strategies for Writing*; and a batch of valuable Cohort Reports. (p. 1)

Susan Drain, an original Inkshedder, illustrated the effectiveness of the newsletter on a personal level for networking, collaborating, and building community. Having been commissioned by her school to look into a writing competency test, Susan used the February 1984 newsletter to petition her Canadian colleagues for their help and expertise. In a follow up in September 1984, she wrote:

> Last winter I requested through *Inkshed* the help of colleagues in my need for information about writing competency testing in universities in Canada. Several of you took the time and trouble to send me most useful materials, and I use *Inkshed* again to thank you all most warmly. My experience proves that this newsletter indeed serves its professed function of linking members of a community in a two-way communication. (p. 2)

This example shows how the newsletter facilitated collaboration and community by acknowledging the role of writing in mutually engaged communication.

From the beginning the newsletter facilitated community. It drew together a geographically diverse set of individuals and provided a forum, through writing, for promoting the teaching of writing and reading in Canada, an opportunity to network, and even some occasional fun. Across the years, however, the *Inkshed* newsletter has become less part of the glue that holds Inkshedders together (as it did in the early years when members eagerly awaited each issue) and more a place for the occasional critique, or thoughtful rumination. Originally a monthly newsletter, it is now published less frequently. One reason it may no longer serve the same role in providing news is new technology. Moving to the forefront, the listserv has become the primary means of communication for the community. Its immediacy means that Inkshedders do not need to wait months between issues for news. It has become a means through which Inkshedders can show their support for colleagues, turn to colleagues for help, pass on information, or even share in a good laugh. The listserv continues to reinforce the values that the community shares. Despite Inkshed's current self-examination, the listserv remains active and an important means of keeping current on what is happening in writing studies in Canada.

My own experience on the listserv illustrates the support that can exist. In my desire to understand the nature of the Inkshed community, I posted a question which resulted in many impassioned responses both to the Inkshed public—in which respondents began communicating directly to each other, rather than directly to me—and a few which came only to me. The postings reflected Inkshedders' expertise and variety of feelings. As well they reflected a sense of support for the community: during one of the busiest times of the year (just before Christmas), Inkshedders took time to affirm that indeed there was a place for Inkshed and inkshedding in Canadian academia.

Others have also reflected on the way the listserv reinforces community values. Betsy Sargent offered the following: "I think the listserv and the website are incredibly valuable in my work—the community exists there as much as or even more than it does at the yearly meeting" (Personal communication, 12/14/2006). Clearly the listserv provided professional support in teaching and research of writing studies in Canada.

Another insight came from a participant who disliked the conference, but valued the listserv. He explained: "I have come to appreciate the virtual community represented in the list. And it isn't the rigor that matters there, it is the community—people who share objectives, understandings, and to some extent values (at least pedagogical)" (Personal communication, 12/14/2006). Thus, by pointing to the shared objectives and values in addition to participation on the listserv, this individual described the listserv as an embodiment of the mutual engagement and joint enterprise of the Inkshed community. These insights also suggest that this technology was a positive force in Inkshed.

Conferences

Print and electronic media supported by the community provided a forum in which to both realize and reinforce academic and social values of the collective. For some, they were the most important tools. While the newsletter and listserv were the means for keeping the community together over a broad geographic expanse throughout the year, a highlight for many and a critical tool for the reinforcing of collective values was the conference. Describing the conference and the values that resonated with her, one person explained: "The informality, diversity of presentation and non-judgmental, constructive spirit—and the people and the fun—kept me coming back" (Inkshedding text, 5/9/2004).

Part of the way that this kind of attitude was facilitated was through the conference format. Typically, conferences were held in isolated settings away from distracting factors such as shopping or sightseeing. Inkshedders had nothing to do but participate in the conference. Furthermore, there were no concurrent sessions. Everyone heard the same presentations, so everyone had the same input. The dialogic engagement was also facilitated by the fact that meals were taken together, everyone was lodged in the same building, and a bar was usually present. This led to late night talks, walks, laughter and other social engagements which fed into friendships and networking on a deeper level. Activities like eating, walking, talking and drinking together in the Inkshed context facilitated knowing people. One person explained this when he wrote: "I found the small retreat setting highly congenial, and found that the ideas of many people there . . . resonated strongly with my own" (Inkshedding text, 5/9/2004). The unique conference setting and format allowed people to connect and participate in meaningful and legitimate ways. This engagement contributed to building and maintaining friendships as affirmed in an inkshedding text: "The conference has become part old friends and part a way to invite new people, often graduate students, into the idea that there IS a community around writing instruction in Canada, however widely spread that community may be" (Inkshedding text, 5/9/2004).

When I worried about attending my first Inkshed conference, my supervisor, Anthony Paré, tried to reassure me that I would enjoy the experience by telling me I would go for walks in the woods with other Inkshedders, sit by the fireplace in my slippers, and otherwise bond and participate in meaningful ways with Inkshedders. While I had no doubt that he had done these things, I remained skeptical that I would have similar experiences. And yet, because so much of what happened at the conference was recurring, I did find that there were woods in which to go for walks—not only did I walk, but I walked with other Inkshedders. I also sat by the fire, and, though not in my slippers, engaged with fellow Inkshedder there as well. These kinds of activities happened repeatedly over the years I attended conferences, reinforcing again and again the values of the collective. The social context and values of the community led to recurring situations.

Another recurring aspect of the conference that contributed to humour, trust, friendship and therefore collegiality (and even the Canadian concern with teaching and language) was the talent show, such as the one I described in the vignette that opened this chapter. On the last night of the conference, Inkshedders pool and share their talents (a term used loosely) with the whole group. The tradition started at the first conference in 1983 when, egged on by

Nan Johnson, Susan Drain sang "Over the Rainbow" (Focus group interview, 5/13/2005), but I would never have really understood the importance of the talent show to community membership without attending and experiencing it for myself. My first talent show was a transformative experience for me and one that woke me up to the phenomenon that was the Inkshed community.

On the one hand, talent night included real talent—singing, reciting poetry, reading short stories, playing musical instruments, and acting. Sometimes this talent was reflective of the kinds of issues that challenge writing teachers—like the woman who shared poems inspired by the struggles she had with her writing students, or a poetry writing activity from a conference session that was then displayed at the talent night. These represented, in a new perspective, some of the issues that resonated with Inkshedders who struggled to make writing meaningful for their students.

On the other hand, most of what went into talent night was silly, fun, and lighthearted. But these crazier acts (like rapping about writing, or Red Green and his nephew Harold using duct tape to instruct students on the finer points of writing) brought humour, trust, and long-lasting friendships.

Practice/Reification of Values

Through the practices of the collective, like the newsletter, listserv, and conference, the values that Inkshedders shared became entrenched or reified in the community. Wenger (1998) explained the way values become reified in a community in the following way:

> I will use the concept of reification very generally to
> refer to the process of giving form to our experiences

by producing objects that congeal this experience into "thingness." In doing so we create points of focus around which the negotiation of meaning becomes organized. (p. 58)

In other words, reification describes processes in which an abstract idea becomes a thing—something more tangible. In the case of the Inkshed community, the values that members shared in pedagogy, research and exchange, along with relationships, were integral to the inkshedding activity itself. As one person explained: "Inkshedding as an activity encapsulates this community's values of collaboration and writing for an audience" (Inkshedding text, 5/9/2004).

Or, as Amanda Goldrick-Jones explained:

Inkshedding [is] the unique, often fruitful, sometimes angsty face-to-face experience at the annual conference. Here, inkshedding morphs into cultural activity, which consolidates community, which gives rise to institutionalisation of tacit and explicit practices and expectations. Newbies must be inculcated. Inculcatees and frequent users find and provide invaluable support. (CASLL Listserv, 12/14/2006)

Or, as Doug Brent explained: "It [inkshedding] is symbolic of a set of attitudes to text, discourse and students that goes well beyond the Inkshed community but is particularly shared by that community: that is, text as interactive doing of some kind" (CASLL Listserv, 12/15/2006). Thus, inkshedding was a defining characteristic of the collective.

Summary

The purpose of this chapter was to explore what it meant to be a member of the Inkshed collective and the strong role of writing in that membership. I have done this by using stories and experiences to look at the values that drew members together, the ways these values were reinforced, and the resulting products of these values that members used. While this has resulted in a somewhat idealized characterization of the community with fewer acknowledgements of some of the more challenging issues, these aspects of the collective help to describe what it meant to be a member of the community. Russ Hunt encapsulated the values, their reinforcement, and the role of inkshedding when he said: "The crucial think [sic] about inkshedding is its social embeddedness—that is, that the writing carries immediate, felt rhetorical force: it's read, read for what it says, and is written with the knowledge that that's going to happen" (CASLL Listserv, 12/15/2006).

This description of inkshedding also describes participation in the collective. Everything that the community valued reinforced Russ's assertion and worked toward its accomplishment. The community valued the teaching of and research into language as a social act (i.e., as meaningful communication); it valued collaboration and friendship. These values were reinforced and facilitated through meaningful dialogic interactions that Russ described as inkshedding. Thus, participation in Inkshed meant being embedded in the collective through the newsletter, listserv and conferences so that interactions had real rhetorical force. They were meaningful and purposeful. What did it mean to be an Inkshedder? It meant, as Roger Graves wrote:

. . . reading the list postings, maybe the newsletter, maybe attending the conference, maybe recognizing who else in your geographical area does work like you do. I think it means you aren't alone—others have had to justify class sizes, too, and they will help you find the resources to help you make your case. I guess it means you will help others and you feel you can also ask for help or ideas if you need them. (CASLL Listserv, 12/13/2006)

But Inkshed membership meant doing these things with the intent that participation would have meaning for the community, with the understanding that language and action have consequences, and with the expectation of mutual engagement through language for the very purpose of being able to use language to engage.

3

Writing Tentatively: Into the Periphery

I n the following three chapters, I explore the process of becoming an Inkshedder and the role that writing plays in helping newcomers join the collective, or move to a place of full participation. One of the challenges of ethnographic research can be gaining access to the research participants. These chapters describe the ways I was able to access the Inkshed community as well as the challenges I faced doing so. The chapters are organized to describe the chronological steps of inkshedding as a framework for a process of becoming a community member—and, as I will discuss in the final chapter, have broader implications for learning in academia and transition into the broad community of academia. Within each of these stages are issues that both hinder and help the transformation to membership. I explore not just the stages of writing, but also parallel these stages to those of becoming an Inkshedder. Each of these stages serves to illustrate significant practices in the Inkshed community that engage its members and hence help to define it as a community of practice. They also reinforce notions that writing is socially situated and support theories of genre (Bazerman, 1994, 2004; Devitt, 2004; Miller, 1984) that argue an interconnectedness between writing practices and the communities that use them.

In this chapter I begin with a vignette that describes my first time attending an Inkshed conference and participating in the inkshedding activity. This is in keeping with theories of autoethnography that seek to join personal with collective experiences (Patton, 2002). I share this experience in an effort to communicate the intensity of attending an Inkshed conference and inkshedding at the conference and have chosen to do so in a narrative form (Clandinin & Connelly, 2000). I also attempt to illustrate the anxiety that permeates inkshedding which a more linguistic, content, or discourse type of analysis of my data would not so effectively communicate. However, this vignette also contributes to an introduction of the initial stage of inkshedding and Inkshed enculturation—or, in other words, the first stages of an Inkshed conference when the process of membership may begin. The activity and conference culture are intricately intertwined. Thus, the data I present in this chapter reflect the initial stages newcomers go through in joining the Inkshed collective by participating in inkshedding. I look first at the sense of vulnerability or exposure that exists in inkshedding. Second, I look at how these feelings of anxiety, which are a predictable element of the practice of inkshedding, are tied to relationships with the community and knowledge of the audience. Finally, I discuss the challenge inherent in the paradox that, in order to know the community one must participate, but, in order to participate, one must feel part of the community. This conundrum provides the potential for facilitating membership. Thus, this chapter is about recognizing the peripheral position of newcomers and the initial participation that facilitates knowing the collective and its values and practices.

Vignette

It's late. At least it feels late to me. 8:20 in the evening after a six-hour drive to Toronto, the subsequent hour driving the back highways of Ontario trying to find the isolated inn, and the sheer exhaustion of the stress of coming to Inkshed for the first time—meeting all these people . . . . I'm exhausted. I would like very much to creep back to my room and go to sleep. Instead, I find myself in a large conference room filled with eight round tables, each with eight chairs. The walls are made from cinder blocks painted a light cream colour in an apparent attempt to brighten an otherwise drab room. The tables are covered with white tablecloths and each has a pitcher of water with eight glasses surrounding it. Pads of paper and pens lie in a loose pile near the water. At the front of the room, Roger and Heather Graves, the keynote speakers, stand behind a long table (also with the requisite white conference room tablecloth) negotiating transparencies for the overhead projector as they talk. And I sit at this corner table working very hard to look like I belong here.

Beside me, Torie [pseudonym] is carefully taking notes on everything that Roger and Heather Graves are saying. I met Torie in line for the dinner buffet. I turned around to introduce myself as we were waiting our turn, and her immediate response was, "Oh, you're the one doing your PhD on inkshedding." I was surprised by her comment. I admitted that I was, but was a little taken aback that this graduate student from Ontario would have heard of me after only an hour of, on my part, unimpressive socializing before dinner.

I was nervous about coming to the conference, and when I first went down to the lounge before supper for the appointed hour of socializing, my stomach was in knots. I'm not great in social situations to begin with. I'm far too shy. I paced my room manically and practically inhaled a large chunk of chocolate to calm my nerves and bolster my courage before I could leave my room. The idea that I was going to walk into this conference as a researcher of the key element of the conference seemed presumptuous. What would people think? How would I get them to accept me?

When I got down to the lounge, I really had to force myself out of my shell and talk to people. I saw Russ Hunt talking animatedly with a group of people—I certainly didn't jump into that conversation. I was far too intimidated by the academic weight and intelligence surrounding me. It was hard too because most people seemed to travel in twos or small groups and on my own I found it difficult to jump into those conversations as well. But every now and then I spotted someone youngish like myself—inevitably a graduate student, or a first-timer at the conference—not hard to spot since we were the ones looking uncomfortable. I forced myself to be friendly and was able to start up a conversation or two that weren't too painful.

I suppose that's why it's easy to talk to Torie. It's her first time at the conference too, and she's also a grad student. But I can't figure out how she can follow Roger and Heather as they talk. Maybe it's because I'm so tired, or because I'm still so new to the field, but I feel as if they're speaking a foreign language. I try to concentrate, but I can't understand a word they're saying. I don't belong here. My mind wanders . . . .

"And so, we'd like to take a few minutes right now to do some inkshedding on that." What? Inkshed right now in the middle of the session? Inkshed about contexts for language use? I don't get it. I don't know what to say. Kenna Manos, an original Inkshedder who introduced herself to me earlier, interrupts both Roger and the complete panic I am feeling about inkshedding.

"Maybe for those who are new, we need to explain what inkshedding is." Roger looks expectantly to Russ to take the lead.

Russ takes the cue, stands and begins to explain. He tells us that inkshedding is a bit like freewriting. Write down whatever thoughts we have. Use writing to make connections, try out new ideas. The important thing, he points out, is that much of what gets written in inkshedding turns out to be garbage and disappears "like the wind." But occasionally, some "gem" will come out of it. Someone from the audience interrupts him to remind him that it's not necessary to sign inksheds. Russ nods and concedes that this writing may remain anonymous. I let a sigh of relief escape—at least if I write something really stupid, no one will know it's me. Russ goes on to explain that after we write we read each other's texts and draw a line in the margin by anything that stands out to us in order to highlight something that others might find worthwhile.

I am new to inkshedding in this context, but I am more or less aware of how it works. It was my introduction to inkshedding in Anthony Paré's WAC class so many years ago that planted the seed for this whole PhD endeavor. Even so, I feel my stomach knotting up and my pulse quickening at the prospect of inkshedding now. If I hadn't known it was coming, the suggestion that we write then and there might have been enough to send me packing. What can I possibly write that might interest this room full of strangers? I remind myself that this is what I'm here for, so I sit at my table and try to look knowledgeable and confident to those around me.

Torie, feeling unsure as well, leans over and whispers to me, "So we just write whatever we want?"

"Basically, yah." I respond. I can see from the look of discomfort on her face that this idea does not sit well with her. She seems to take a long time looking for the pen that had been in her hand, finding a fresh

sheet of paper, and carefully labeling it with the date, time, names of the speakers, and the title of their presentation.

Slowly we all start to write. I suspect that I am not the only one at the table feigning confidence. Three of us at the table are graduate students and have had the chance to talk over dinner. Two other people sit at the table writing with us. They introduced themselves as they sat down, but I have no idea who they are or what their relationship to the Inkshed community is. As we write, two other women slip into the room, negotiate their way to our table, and begin to write as well. They seem confident as they take up pen and paper and not at all stymied by the task they have walked in on. I assume they have been here before.

I've come to appreciate a lot of things about inkshedding, but I'm not sure I'll ever enjoy the anxiety of writing something intelligent on the spot. And in this context, I am hyper-aware of having to write something intelligent that makes me appear to have something worthwhile to contribute to this community. I try to remind myself of what Russ said—that much of what we write is garbage, that I don't have to come up with anything brilliant. That momentarily takes away some of the anxiety and I am able to start writing. I am somehow also aware that if we are all new at the table and we all hang back, then the inkshedding won't work. Someone has to take the lead and jump in. So I write, drawing confidence from the fact that I've done this before and survived. I pass my paper to the centre of the table to be read.

For several reasons I chose to begin this chapter with a vignette describing my first time attending an Inkshed conference and inkshedding there. Primarily, I wanted to bring the reader into the Inkshed experience by recreating, through this vignette, the thoughts, feelings, and activities that many people who attend the Inkshed

55

conference for the first time experience. I included the first time inkshedding and first time attending a conference together, because I believe that the activity and conference are interconnected. Because of the values reciprocated through them, the activity facilitates the conference and the conference facilitates the activity. By presenting the practice and context through personal narrative, I hope to evoke a sense of resonance.

In this chapter I examine the feelings of anxiety and vulnerability that haunt many newcomers who find themselves on the periphery of a community, unsure of how to participate. I begin by looking at feelings that newcomers experience in order to illustrate the depth and profundity of the angst that they may feel. I then explore some of the social reasons for this angst. Drawing on theories of genre that help to explain the way writing practices are dependent on social context, and theories of communities of practice (CoPs) that explain collective practices, I present data suggesting that feelings of anxiety and vulnerability are connected to newcomers' desire to respond in a way that will enable mutual engagement with the collective. While some may recognize the exigence of the rhetorical moment (i.e., the need for a particular response at a particular moment), they may lack confidence in their literacy practices and question their ability to participate appropriately. Some of the challenges newcomers face in their attempts to engage include learning unwritten rules and understanding community members and their values. The anxiety and vulnerability that accompany a position of peripherality have various consequences. On the one hand, they can lead to such intense fear that a newcomer simply does not participate, or, on the other hand, as newcomers recognize how the activity puts everyone in a potentially vulnerable position, this recognition can be a catalyst for moving to a position of more active participation.

Vulnerability

As newcomers engage in inkshedding, they draw on what Barton and Hamilton (2005) described as common literacy practices (ways of using language symbols in particular situations) to facilitate their participation. Typically, newcomers have generalized practices that they can draw on to function in inkshedding, such as familiarity with freewriting or knowledge of the language of the discourse of composition studies. For some, however, inkshedding may be so foreign that background knowledge of practices is insufficient. Thus, unsure of how to engage or respond, newcomers may feel vulnerable. This was true of both my first time inkshedding and my first time attending an Inkshed conference. Unfamiliar with both situations, I worried about the outcomes, or how my writing and I would be accepted.

In the years since my initial participation, I have used autoethnography (Ellis & Bochner, 2000) and narrative inquiry (Clandinin & Connelly, 2000) to think and write about my extreme anxiety (Horne, 2004). I wanted to know if I was alone in these feelings of trepidation, or if others could relate to what I was feeling and had also experienced vulnerability. I explored this question through interim writing (Clandinin & Connelly, 2000) in which I used writing as discovery. I took my ruminations to participants of an Inkshed conference and found that my experiences resonated in a powerful way with what other participants had gone through. I was struck by the force of the language that others used to describe their initial inkshedding experiences. In this section, I share the results of working between my experiences and the narratives shared by Inkshedders. The following excerpts from inkshedding texts illustrate the common feeling of vulnerability. I have added italics to the words describing vulnerability in order to highlight the extremity of the feelings:

I reacted with *fear* and *trepidation*, assuming critical eyes would fall on my writing. I seriously *doubted* my ability to write anything significant, anything of value to those I was sharing my writing with. (Inkshedding text, 5/9/2004)

I remember being *nervous* about having others [read] my work—I'm not used to sharing my thoughts. (Inkshedding text, 5/9/2004)

I was out there, *vulnerable, naked* . . . . (Inkshedding text, 5/9/2004)

. . . I felt very *nervous*—the notion of "publication" and the making public of my "writing" created real *anxiety*. (Inkshedding text, 5/9/2004)

I didn't like it—I felt *pressure* to say something intelligent. (Inkshedding text, 5/9/2004)

There is something *intimidating* about the first time being asked to Inkshed, not because we don't have responses to share, but because of our *feelings of inadequacy* when it comes to our own writing. That seems ludicrous to be coming from a teacher of writing, but writing for peers differs with regard to social context—are we "good enough" to be involved in this inkshedding community? Will people think we have nothing to contribute? Will our credibility stand up to scrutiny? All of these questions reflect our (my?)

sense of inadequacy when it comes to my own writing. (Inkshedding text, 5/9/2004)

Discomfort. Fear that I had nothing to say that anyone would want to hear. (Inkshedding text, 5/9/2004)

As a newcomer to the Inkshed community I also *worried* about my ability to respond intelligently to the issues being presented. (Inkshedding text, 5/9/2004)

I felt *uncomfortable* (kind of *exposed* without any desire to do so). (Inkshedding text, 5/9/2004)

I remember feeling *vulnerable*. (Inkshedding text, 5/9/2004)

. . . for many writing is *exposure, vulnerability, danger*. (Inkshedding text, 5/9/2004)

I experienced some *discomfort, fear of exposure* . . . [ellipsis his/hers] (Inkshedding text, 5/9/2004)

I was totally *intimidated*, felt like an outsider who had been extended a polite but weak invitation to join an exclusive club. (Inkshedding text, 5/9/2004)

Fear, trepidation, intimidated, inadequate, vulnerable—these descriptors illustrate and express the intense feelings associated with inkshedding. The examples are important because they acknowledge and describe a shared experience—discomfort in being asked to fully participate even though newcomers are still in a peripheral position. As Lave and Wenger (1991) pointed out, learning and participation is a process that requires a gradual increase in responsibility. It is also typically facilitated by a mentoring program that helps newcomers negotiate expectations and responsibility. Newcomers to Inkshed have a variety of ways in which they can choose to participate—from presentations to talent night to simply socializing. Inkshedding, however, is expected of everyone. It is the one act in which everyone—including newcomers—participates.

Although immediate inkshedding is expected, newcomers rarely have the benefit of mentorship. For example, one veteran Inkshedder contributed to "The Wall" (a graffiti board set up at a conference) a description of her first inkshedding experience and the importance of having extra explanations through a seasoned Inkshedder. She wrote: "Jim Reither + Pat Dias did keynote (I think!) that was my first formal intro to inkshedding. However, I didn't grasp how to do it until Rick Coe explained at our "small group" table" (The Wall, Inkshed XX, 2003). This example demonstrates the importance of a mentor, but, as my own experience showed in the vignette that opened this chapter, without the benefit of a mentor insecurities can surface as newcomers negotiate expectations for participation on their own. Only the opportunity for anonymity lessens the weight of participation.

Anonymity

One of the ways that the creators of inkshedding and conference organizers try to facilitate newcomer participation in inkshedding is by allowing inkshedding texts to be circulated anonymously. That is, writers are not required to identify their writing with their name. Lave and Wenger (1991), in their explanation of legitimate peripheral participation (LPP), described how participation in the community must be real and meaningful. Furthermore, newcomers participate in the activities with less responsibility or fewer consequences. Allowing participants to take part in inkshedding without signing their text invites them to take risks and open themselves to vulnerability in a way that would not otherwise be possible. It allows participants to take risks without fear of personal reprisal.

In a personal interview, I explored this perspective with Anthony Paré. He explained the opportunities and the potential that anonymity affords:

> Anthony: The anonymity for me, I remember it forcing me to think beyond what I might have thought ordinarily—it pushed me to write about things, to think about things, that were not just typical or knee jerk, or bland, or cliché. It forced you to say, to say something that might be unusual, or might be a different way of looking at it. Or brought up perspective that maybe nobody else could write.
>
> Miriam: That came out because of the anonymity?
>
> Anthony: I think so. Well, it came out because of the invitation. An invitation does that. Anonymity may give you the freedom or the security to do it where you might not do it elsewhere. The invitation to speak is always the invitation to say something that is worth hearing. Someone says, "Well, what do you think?" And you've got an opening to say something that might or might not be worth hearing or listening to, but then if someone says "What do you think?" and you don't know who **you** are, then it gives you not only the invitation to speak, but

> possibly the invitation to go way out on a limb,
> to take a chance, to try some ideas on that if they
> knew who was speaking you might be less willing
> to try on. (12/5/2006)

To paraphrase, anonymity allows participants to advance ideas and participate in a meaningful way with the rest of the community without worrying that they will not be taken seriously because they may be new to the community, graduate students, or in other ways on the periphery. It is a way of democratizing the experience so that everyone has the opportunity to be heard. While anonymity in inkshedding continues to be a topic of debate (some feel that unauthored discourse is never appropriate and may in fact lead to personal attacks, which I discuss in the next section), it does provide a way for newcomers to participate in the activity without taking on the same kind of responsibility in the activity as someone like Russ Hunt, an original Inkshedder, who always signs his name. For some, anonymity provides the security newcomers need to be able to engage.

Despite the opportunities that anonymity may provide, it does not necessarily entirely take away that anxiety and vulnerability of the experience. The following section of this chapter explores how newcomers negotiate their participation by measuring themselves against the collective and trying to understand the collective.

Responding to the Collective

As Barton and Hamilton (2005) argued, literacy events are embedded within social dynamics. In this study, the inkshedding activity takes place within a rich cultural context of values and practices—some explicit, some implicit. I described these values in the previous chapter as caring about teaching, research, and use of language in a Canadian setting, and forming personal relationships with colleagues in the pursuit of these values. This concept of the social dynamics surrounding literacy events is also similar to understanding rhetorical context as understood by genre theorists because language use is dependent on things like goals, audience, and rationale. In addition, as I explained in Chapter 1 in my discussion of CoPs and LPP, in order to gain membership in a community, newcomers must have opportunities to participate in meaningful ways. My data suggest that lack of familiarity with the social structures or rhetorical context (namely, the audience, purposes, and exigence for writing) within which inkshedding is embedded contributes to anxiety and vulnerability.

As Wenger (1998) pointed out, for newcomers to become full participants in the community and the activity, their participation must be mutually engaging, lead to joint enterprise, and engage them in shared repertoire in a collaborative way. Thus, in the collective inkshedding activity, participation must be mutually engaging for both the writer and the collective, and lead to a common purpose to further the discussion of teaching and language. The challenge for the newcomer then is in finding appropriate ways to engage with the collective or audience by finding appropriate ways to respond to the common prompt (the initial stage of inkshedding).

In this section, I describe the importance of knowing the community and the audience for whom one is writing in order to begin to engage with the collective. I do so by exploring the challenges newcomers face when learning the nature of the collective and in engaging with the collective.

Learning the Collective

Because newcomers have chosen to attend an academic conference on writing, there is an assumption that they share, at the very least, common background knowledge about academic writing. However, the Inkshed collective embodies much more than this. As discussed in Chapter 2, it is concerned not just with background knowledge of scholarly work in writing studies or composition pedagogy, but also with reflective practices that create knowledge. Community practices like inkshedding reflect this, but these are characteristics of the collective that newcomers must learn. On arrival, many newcomers quickly learn that Inkshed is a culture; it is a set of values, beliefs and practices.

One Inkshedder, now well established in the community, reflected on the nature of the community as he described his first time inkshedding as trying to carry on a conversation with someone whose culture or background he did not know. He explained it in the following way:

> I guess my first experience inkshedding was that it resembled other written conversations I had been engaged in, mostly personal, sometimes professional. The only difference is that it was a hybrid of personal/ private writing, and writing for a small society whose members and ethos and values I did not yet know. (Inkshedding text, 5/9/2004)

This excerpt shows a recognition that the community had a set of beliefs that was unknown to the newcomer but not totally unfamiliar. He made sense of this new literacy event by drawing parallels to other literacy practices, both personal and professional, but acknowledged something new to learn.

Another participant also recognized the distinct nature of Inkshed—learning new values made manifest through writing. She described the experience as having to learn a new genre. She explained:

> First experience of inkshedding occurred for me at Inkshed last year. As is usual in using a new genre, I did not have much idea of what an "inkshed" would look like, nor did I really know why the inkshedding process worked. As a newcomer to the Inkshed community, I also worried about my ability to respond intelligently to the issues being presented. (Inkshedding text, 5/9/2004)

Part of this excerpt describes how not knowing the genre of inkshedding (i.e., the collective values and practices that have led to the relative stability of this writing activity at conferences) contributed to an anxiety about identifying with the community. In other words, learning a new genre required learning a new set of values and beliefs and how to incorporate those in writing. Lack of familiarity with the social context led to insecurity in the writing task.

The experience of learning to inkshed can be frustrating if one does not know the audience for whom one is writing. This awareness of not knowing exactly who the audience is or what the audience values permeates many anxiety-filled experiences. It impacts the way participants feel about inkshedding and therefore their participation in the inkshedding activity.

Consider again some of the passages I used earlier to illustrate the vulnerable feelings associated with inkshedding. Each of the writers in these excerpts qualified how they felt about their inkshedding experiences by referencing the community and reflecting a concern with the ability to identify with the collective. One writer described the first time inkshedding in the following way: "Discomfort. Fear that I had nothing to say that anyone would want to hear" (Inkshedding text, 5/9/2004).

In this example the writer expressed a fear not of remaining mute or lacking the ability to express ideas, but that no one would want to listen to the ideas. The fear, therefore, is not that there is nothing to say, but rather, whether or not it is worth paying attention to in this particular setting. In other words, the writer wants to be able to identify with the community, but not knowing enough about the ways in which others will respond, worries about remaining on the periphery of, or even outside of, the collective. If unable to engage meaningfully with the audience, then one could not move to a place of full participation. (This is why publication, as described in Chapter 5, is such an important part of the process.) Other Inkshedders made similar attempts to find ways to engage with the community. One person wrote: "I reacted with fear and trepidation, assuming critical eyes would fall on my writing. I seriously doubted my ability to write anything significant, anything of value to those I was sharing my writing with" (Inkshedding text, 5/9/2004). Another wrote: "I was aware, in some ways of trying to please my readers, to write something significant or meaningful, something that would pique the interest (laughter, philosophical pondering, etc.) of my readers" (Inkshedding text, 5/9/2004).

The first of these two examples echoed the feelings of vulnerability described previously. The participants, driven by anxiety, feared a negative reception by the community, or an inability to engage.

The writers in both of these excerpts went on to question their ability to function in a meaningful way within the community. The language reflects this. The sentences do not end with "significant" or "meaningful." Instead, both qualified what they meant by the word "significant." They redefined it for this context to mean something valuable or worthwhile to the audience. Thus, the writers were not concerned with having an idea to write about, but rather, how that idea would resonate with the collective.

One final example illustrates the experience of worrying about meaningful engagement of the writer with the community: "I felt a desire to write something impressive that would confirm my ability to function within this academic community that was new to me" (Inkshedding text, 5/9/2004). Instead of using the word "significant" like the previous two examples, this writer explained the desire to write something "impressive." The writer followed the same pattern as the previous two examples and redefined "impressive" to reflect how the writer negotiated entry into the community. The fear and vulnerability that some individuals experience in inkshedding is not a result of a complete mental blank or inability to express themselves. Instead, it reflects the writers' concern with audience—in this case, the Inkshed community—and whether or not the writing will resonate and have meaning for the audience. It reflects a fear of being left on the periphery as newcomers trying to engage with the collective.

Challenges to Engagement

The difficult experiences that newcomers face when trying to make connections with the collective are not entirely self-generated. Rather, some aspects of the collective contribute to the challenges newcomers encounter. These include implicit rules, the complex multidisciplinary makeup of the community, and resulting conversations.

i. Rules

A challenge that faces newcomers as they try to identify with the collective are all the unwritten rules associated with inkshedding. As Rick Coe explained: "There's a sense of, not so much that there's a right way to do it, as there are wrong ways to do it, that there are things that people might do to make it not work" (Focus group interview, 5/13/2005). Anthony Paré confirmed the existence of implicit rules. He said: "There is a right way of going about doing this [inkshedding] and there is a wrong way" (Personal interview, 12/5/2006). At each conference, when participants receive initial instructions, they never hear what *not* to do. Instead, cursory instructions tell them to write whatever they wish. Only through trial and error do writers come to understand what things work in inkshedding and what things do not.

It is worth mentioning, as well, however, that it is also through trial and error that the community itself learns what works and does not work. For example, no time frame has ever been established for producing published inkshedding texts after they have been circulated. However, at one conference, when these texts were not produced until the following day when the presentations they reflected on were no longer fresh, it became clear that an immediate turnaround was necessary if the inkshedding activity was going to be dialogic and reinvest the published ideas into ongoing conversations. (The event, in fact, led Russ Hunt to revise his 2004 article "What is Inkshedding?").

Russ Hunt described one problem that occurs in inkshedding if people write their texts as personal letters to the presenter. Misunderstanding the literacy event, they draw on inappropriate literacy practices to participate. He explained that by inkshedding as writing personal letters, participants do not understand the larger context of what they are doing (although this larger context is rarely expressed, let alone explained). While the purpose of inkshedding is to advance discussions (something that newcomers often do not understand until they have seen the published texts), writing a personal letter effectively closes a discussion by blocking out other participants. In addition, accolades for a job well done also end the conversation. Russ explained:

> "Thanks Dorothy, I liked it" is goodbye. And many of the kinds of inksheds that I'm talking about are evaluative and final. The problem with them . . . is that they exclude other people, it's that they . . . don't have built into them a kind of further invitation to respond either from that person or from somebody else. (Focus group interview, 5/13/2005)

Newcomers face the challenge of interpreting the rhetorical context and responding appropriately even though rules are not explicit. They must carefully read the setting and guess at the appropriateness of their responses. They do so with varied degrees of success.

ii. Multidisciplinarity

Another one of the challenges to newcomers' appropriate participation is the diverse makeup of the community. Inkshed tends to be multidisciplinary. While trying to describe the Inkshed community, Russ Hunt said:

> We don't come from the same disciplinary context. One of the things about Inkshed from the beginning . . . is that . . . we've got people from psych departments, we've got people from English departments, we've got people from education faculties, we've got people from

writing centres, we've got high school teachers . . . .
(Focus group interview, 5/13/2005)

While Russ saw this variety as a positive characteristic of the community because it allows for multiple viewpoints, it can also be disconcerting for newcomers trying to understand the audience for whom they are writing. In the vignette that opened this chapter, I described my experience inkshedding at an Inkshed conference for the first time. In that situation, I was very much aware that I did not know all the other people who were going to read what I wrote. I knew the two other graduate students with whom I was sitting and so initially had them in mind as my audience as I wrote. However, because I knew the process, and that others in the room might eventually read my writing, I had to try to imagine the rest of the audience. The only other person I knew in the room was Ann Beer, a professor at McGill who was influential in my graduate work. I used her, and my background relationship with her, as a model for the rest of the community and kept her at the back of my mind as my imagined audience as I wrote. However, by using her as my focus, I did not account for the people who were high school teachers, from psychology departments, or even writing centre people. The challenge is finding some common ground that will resonate with all of the different backgrounds represented at the conference.

Clearly, newcomers to Inkshed must work through many complexities in order to understand the community for whom they write. It is not surprising that so many feel exposed and vulnerable as they try to negotiate through these various unknowns.

iii. Conversations

Despite the fact that Inkshedders come from a variety of backgrounds, the conversations that go on at Inkshed are relatively focused, and highly academic. Some people never manage to engage in the kinds of discussions taking place in Inkshed simply because they are part of other academic conversations that do not overlap with the Inkshed conversation. One long time Inkshedder explained this phenomenon as it occurred with people he brought to the conference. He said:

> I think one of the problems that we had is that the level of conversation we have, I think, is relatively academic. And I know that I have brought [elementary] teachers and high school teachers a couple of times to conferences and they've never come back. And the reason they've never come back is because we're not having the same conversation that they're having. And never will have the same conversations. I don't quite know why not. (Focus group interview, 5/13/2005)

Russ Hunt confirmed this observation with his own description of an occasional conference-goer. He explained:

> [She] has a lot of problems with inkshedding because she feels like an impostor at it, and it's partly because we're having a conversation that [she's] right on the edge of. She has other conversations—equally valuable, equally important. But I mean, I'll say, 'Well, are you going to come this year?' and, 'Well, no, I don't think so.' Sometimes she'll come and enjoy it, and learn stuff, but it's not really her conversation. (Focus group interview, 5/13/2005)

This Inkshed conversation is best described through the Burkean parlour metaphor. In describing the way knowledge is created in disciplinary communities, Burke (1941) envisioned the following scene:

> Imagine that you enter a parlor. You come late. When you arrive, others have long preceded you, and they are engaged in a heated discussion, a discussion too heated for them to pause and tell you exactly what it is about. In fact, the discussion had already begun long before any of them got there, so that no one present is qualified to retrace for you all the steps that had gone before. You listen for a while, until you decide that you have caught the tenor of the argument; then you put in your oar. Someone answers; you answer him; another comes to your defense; another aligns himself against you, to either the embarrassment or gratification of your opponent, depending upon the quality of your ally's assistance. However, the discussion is interminable. The hour grows late, you must depart. And you do depart, with the discussion still vigorously in progress. (pp. 110-111)

Like Burke's conversation, the Inkshed conversation is ongoing and located within its own parlour, its set of cultural and social circumstances. Some Inkshedders recognize the uniqueness of the conversation and might try to explain newcomers' lack of participation by suggesting that the conversation is uninteresting to them because of its academic level. Others interpret the conversation differently and criticize it as being too "exclusive and lacking in intellectual rigor—almost superficial" (Personal communication, 12/15/2006), or as being "boring, . . . ingrown and insular" (Personal communication, 12/14/2006). Regardless of the interpretation one gives to the kind of conversation Inkshedders are having, it is clear that the nature of the conversation either excites or engages some, but not others.

Despite the fact that some people either fail to learn or choose to ignore implicit rules, adapt to the multidisciplinary nature of the community, engage in the overarching discourse of the group, or otherwise interpret the Inkshed audience, others have successfully come to know the audience for whom they write through trial and error. Knowing the audience facilitates the inkshedding process and hence participation in the entire collective. Having a clearer understanding of the rhetorical context, a participant is able to write more appropriately and therefore engage with the collective. The ability to engage with the collective facilitates membership because, as Wenger (1998) explained, communities result from mutually engaged-in practices. A long-time Inkshedder helped to illustrate the importance of knowing the audience for whom you write in inkshedding. He explained that for him, although he does not particularly enjoy the inkshedding activity, he is able to do it because he knows his audience. He pointed to people like Russ Hunt, Kenna Manos, Nan Johnson, Rick Coe, and others who have been attending for many years as the audience for whom he writes. He explained:

> Part of the problem that I've gotten better at is that I now have a sense of audience that I never had before. And that sense of audience is the other people around this table in many ways. They're not the initiates there. And so, you know, we've developed a kind

of community. And so when I write, I write to that community. (Focus group interview, 5/13/2005)

The experience that this Inkshedder described represents what many have come to learn: knowing the Inkshed community facilitates the inkshedding process. However, it is not always easy to know the audience. Sometimes, learning what the community values must come through trial and error in the inkshedding practice and other interactions with the community.

Consequences

One of the great ironies of Inkshed is that in order to be able to fully, or successfully, participate in the community and the activity, individuals must understand the nature of the collective and the unwritten rules. However, that understanding comes through the act of participation. The anxiety that occurs as a result of lack of familiarity with these challenges has a range of consequences from complete non-participation on the one hand, to total participation on the other, and everything in between.

Non-Participation

I was struck by the story of one graduate student who described her introduction to inkshedding, which took place not at a conference but in a graduate course. She explained that she was so intimidated by sharing her writing that she carefully folded up her inkshedding text and hid it in her pocket when it came time to share what she had written. She explained:

1st Inkshed experience was part of a language studies course, led by an instructor who is part of the Inkshed community. At the time, it felt awkward as I didn't see the value of this exercise, but even more telling, I didn't want my classmates to read my [emphasis hers] writing. So while I did inkshed, I didn't tape my paper on the wall. (Inkshedding text, 5/9/2004)

In the situation this student described, inkshedding was enacted in one of the ways common in the early days of inkshedding. Rather than circulating writing around small groups, all inkshedding texts were taped to the walls around the classroom so that everyone could read them. In describing this method of circulating texts, Anthony Paré wrote: "I remember that the image used as a comparison . . . was on Chinese newspapers that were posted publicly, and that attracted crowds" (Personal correspondence, 4/1/2007).

Although the student participated by reading her classmates' inkshedding, she did not experience the full potential of inkshedding because her own text was not circulated. She did not fully participate and thus was unable to learn all she could have about the collective in which she was participating, or contribute to the collective in any significant way. This kind of experience is reminiscent of what happens in classrooms. When students feel uncomfortable or threatened, they may simply miss class or not do an assignment. One student I had in a writing class confessed that she always skipped the classes the previous semester in which she had to do peer reviews.

This lack of participation is not limited to students in a classroom. I have watched individuals at conferences conveniently slip out of the door of the conference room when it came time to inkshed—some with the excuse that they could not wait any longer for their cigarette or bathroom break, others, more blatant, that they did not want to inkshed.

By not participating, individuals not only fail to learn more about the collective, they also fail to engage in the community in a way that is meaningful to the collective. As discussed in Chapter 2, inkshedding is the embodiment of collective values. Non-participation suggests a disconnect with those values, and therefore, a separation from membership. The non-participation I am referring to is not just the occasional removal from the activity because of a tired hand, mental exhaustion (as is common at the end of conferences), replacement with oral discussion, or other common happenings among many Inkshedders. Rather, I am referring to those who come for the first time and refuse to participate, or those who come periodically to conferences, but fail to engage with the collective. Even when the overt non-participation is done deliberately, the result is the same: the individuals are not members of the collective.

Limited Participation

Similar to people who simply refuse to participate are those who are so anxious when they write that they write something that is so safe it borders on boring. Anthony Paré explained that fear leads people to uninteresting responses. He said: "If you were too timid, you couldn't write or would write bland stuff" (Personal interview, 12/5/2006). Bland writing, like no writing, fails to engage the collective. Like the student who does not participate, this failure to engage also resonates with classroom experiences where students hand in writing assignments that meet technical requirements, but fail to push ideas or take ownership for new or unique thinking. As Lave and Wenger (1991) pointed out in their discussion of LPP, without meaningful engagement, learning does not take place and the newcomer cannot move to a position of fuller participation.

While some excuse themselves from participation, or participate blandly, others will engage, but do so with resistance and unhappily. Consider the following comment: "I comply with this experience that is forced on me, but it is certainly uncomfortable" (Inkshedding text, 5/9/2004). Because this particular inkshedding text was submitted to me anonymously, I was unable to follow up with the individual who expressed these feelings. However, the language of the comment implies that the writer did not willingly participate in inkshedding, and that the experience was unpleasant. Thus I believe that, like the student who did not participate, or a newcomer who responded in clichés or vagaries, the attitude of this writer also precluded full participation in the inkshedding activity, and therefore in the collective. By that I mean that the writer was unlikely to take risks, advance edgy ideas, or really engage in meaningful dialogic interaction. Again, Lave and Wenger's (1991) ideas are appropriate here. Participation must be meaningful.

Like the writer who complies but is unhappy doing so, there are other people in the community who consider themselves Inkshedders but do not particularly enjoy the activity. One long-time Inkshedder expressed his feelings about inkshedding in the following way:

> I didn't—and still don't find the act of inkshedding especially powerful either way. I recognize its value and do it dutifully, and have never been intimidated by sharing my writing. But the published inksheds seem stale by the time I see them, and I find the whole exercise takes away time that I personally would rather use for discussion. (Inkshedding text, 5/9/2004)

Although this Inkshedder can see potential merit in the activity, and participates without argument, he is unmoved by the experience. In further discussions with this individual, it was clear that he felt that the Inkshed community would continue to grow even if inkshedding were not a part of it.

Inappropriate Participation

One of the potential problems of feeling vulnerable or exposed in a situation like inkshedding is the potential for abuse as a defensive mechanism. As one original Inkshedder explained:

> One of the things that I think happens in [this] community is that what people have in common is caring strongly about what they do. Strongly enough to be vulnerable in this kind of interchange. And when they're vulnerable, they can be threatened, and that's when the trashing comes in. (Focus group interview, 5/13/2005)

In the early years of inkshedding as people had to grapple with the new genre and way of thinking that inkshedding required, this insecurity and lack of understanding sometimes led to uncomfortable situations in which people were "trashed," criticized, or otherwise felt the brunt of disparagement. As one original Inkshedder explained: "Trashing came when an idea that questioned some solid assumptions was advanced" (Personal communication, 2/28/2006).

Or as Russ Hunt explained:

> It has to do with the nature of inkshedding. My view now is that it was a proto-example of "flaming" via

email. Inkshedding was email before there was email. People who inkshedded after sessions sometimes didn't actually understand (à la email) that this was dialogic discourse—and people who read negative comments about presentations sometimes over reacted to the negativity. There was no slot in anybody's rhetorical world for writing in that functional social situation. The genre was undergoing invention. (Personal email, 2/5/2006)

As Russ described, people lacked the literacy practices necessary to engage in the inkshedding practice and responded with other literacy practices. They failed to understand the rhetorical exigence. Thus, although "trashing" is not considered acceptable in the current Inkshed environment, it has existed in the past and seems to always remain a concern because the underlying conditions that fostered "trashing" in early years may yet emerge from those unfamiliar with the genre.

Participation as Engagement

While there appear to be many negative consequences of feeling anxious or vulnerable in inkshedding, there are also more positive outcomes. For some who began their Inkshed experience feeling fearful, they were able to persevere and eventually move beyond that initial discomfort. In my own experience inkshedding, although I occasionally felt some discomfort when it came time to write, I eventually came to be able to write without fear of what the community would think of me. Similarly, I felt confident taking part in the conference as both a presenter and talent night participant. While the reasons for this will be explained in more depth in the following two chapters, I attribute it to a willingness to continue through the initial discomfort of the inkshedding and Inkshed experience. While the community was willing to engage with newcomers, the newcomers had to be equally willing to engage with the collective. By participating in inkshedding, newcomers were potentially able to engage in meaningful ways with the collective. Nonparticipation or reluctant participation did not facilitate the same meaningful engagement.

Other participants shared this perspective. In a similar account, another Inkshed participant shared the feeling of intimidation and discomfort with the inkshedding process upon first exposure to it. The participant then went on to explain, however, that by the end of the weekend, those feelings of vulnerability had disappeared. The participant wrote:

> I went to Inkshed 19 in PEI in 2002 and knew very little about the Inkshed process. I remember being nervous about having others [read] my work—I'm not used to sharing my thoughts. However, I did find I enjoyed the process and any vulnerability I felt at the start was gone by the end of the conference. Now I don't feel any hesitation about writing at all and truly enjoy reading what others have to say. (Inkshedding text, 5/9/2004)

This example illustrates how after going through the process of inkshedding throughout an entire weekend, the writer got over the feelings of vulnerability and was able to enjoy participating. One other participant shared a similar experience:

> My first experience of inkshedding was to prepare a piece of writing that reflected a change in discourse. As

I'm not teaching English, I used a personal experience
of writing. I was very excited about the insights the
writing produced, but, at the same time, nervous that
the writing might not be appropriate for the group. My
fears were to diminish over the three days however as
I realized that I did have ideas to share. (Inkshedding
text, 5/9/2004)

These participants came to understand, through their inkshedding
experience, that the community was accepting of them and that their
ideas were validated. As a result, they lost their feelings of fear and
vulnerability and engaged enthusiastically in participation.

One final example provides a rich analogy for describing the ways
that participating, despite discomfort, helps Inkshedders engage with
the collective. Brock MacDonald, a well-established Inkshedder,
described his process of learning to inkshed in the following way:

1st time inkshedding—the horror! The horror! I was not
keen, to put it mildly. I was used to the conventional
conference paper aftermath, i.e., the situation in
which one has the option of speaking up and posing
a question or raising an issue, and one also has the
option of remaining silent. Writing my responses
on the spot and sharing them made me feel naked,
essentially defenseless, vulnerable.

Initiation into the inkshedding community followed
almost immediately on the sense of vulnerability I
just described. "hmm—everyone else is in the same
boat—it's ok!" Feeling of horror gave way rapidly to
a feeling of liberation. The metaphor of nakedness

is actually important here—on, say, Wreck Beach in Vancouver, one quickly finds that same sense of liberation. Everybody's naked—big deal. Everyone's writing—big deal. (Inkshedding text, 5/9/2004)

Brock's analogy of nakedness reflects the fears that others I have discussed in this chapter also expressed. It also shows how those who are able to let go of their fears and participate are able to engage with the collective—to move beyond their own insecurities. Brock described how participants, by recognizing discomfort but participating anyway, are able to move to a position of more meaningful participation in inkshedding.

Although the scope of this research was not to look at the personality traits of those who attended Inkshed conferences, the variety of responses that this data evoked suggests that participants had a huge range of interests, abilities, and beliefs. Further, as Bourdieu (1977) explained in his work on habitus, attributes such as knowledge, skills, and values are the result of conditioning or experience. The variety here implies that some people were more predisposed than others to engage in the Inkshed community. Everyone had the same context for the experience and yet individuals reacted in different ways, suggesting that background experience played a role in how well newcomers were able to integrate into the collective.

Summary

In this chapter I have described the ways in which inkshedding and joining the Inkshed collective could be a vulnerable experience. Participants felt exposed and fearful because they were unsure how they would be able to engage with the collective. This experience serves to test the theory of communities of practice (CoPs) as described by Wenger (1998) to acknowledge personal anxieties and insecurities that newcomers face in joining a CoP. Although Wenger accounted for social interactions, he failed to incorporate the ways in which feelings of insecurity may influence participation in a community. My data suggest that although not universal, feelings of vulnerability are common and the ways individuals deal with these feelings will have repercussions for the ways that they interact and engage with community members, and therefore, ultimately, with community membership.

In addition, engagement is made more complicated by unwritten rules, a multidisciplinary community, and a relatively focused kind of conversation that takes place. Thus, mutual engagement may be more difficult to achieve than Wenger's (1998) model might suggest. While Wenger seemed to imply that common goals and practices would naturally lead to mutual engagement, this experience suggests that understanding not just the goals but the culture and values that drive those goals influences participation. In this case, cultural values hidden in unwritten rules, for example, frustrated an individual's ability to mutually engage.

This observation is perhaps better understood through genre theory that links writing practices to social values. The ability to recognize social values—and when and how to respond appropriately in an inkshedding text—exemplifies the exigence that genre theorists (Bazerman, 1994; Berkenkotter & Huckin, 1995; Miller, 1984) described. Part of the appropriateness of response lies in using correct or appropriate language. Again, as Barton and Tusting (2005) pointed out, Wenger's lack of attention to language is a weakness in his theory. The description of how language can or should be used in this discussion of vulnerability highlights the importance of literacy events in the social dynamics of CoPs.

Vulnerability can have a multitude of consequences—from non-participation to full participation. As a researcher, I recognized immediately the need to participate. Although it was uncomfortable for me and filled me with dread, I did participate both in the inkshedding activity and the Inkshed community. Without that participation, I would have failed to arrive at the membership I now claim. In the following chapter I explain how I participated, that is, I make the comparison that my participation in the community was like an inkshed text circulating during the inkshedding activity. Recognizing that some people feel unable to participate, I explore the position that Brock MacDonald described. I look at the ways that those who are able to push through the vulnerability are able to participate and how that participation helps them move toward a position of membership in the collective.

4

Sharing Texts:
Moving Beyond the Edges

I n the first step of the inkshedding process, participants quickly
write in response to a common prompt such as a presentation
or a reading. To some, particularly newcomers, writing this
way is an exposure of the self that makes them feel uncomfortable
because they do not know the audience for whom they are writing.
Therefore, they worry about how readers will respond to the text. This
phenomenon illustrates the socially situated nature of writing and
also exemplifies the ways that learning takes place through practice
known as legitimate peripheral participation (LPP) (Lave & Wenger,
1991). Newcomers are asked to participate in a meaningful way by
inkshedding with the community. Participating in this way provides
one kind of opportunity to learn community values and engage in
common goals with the collective (however challenging that may be).

In this chapter, keeping in mind the socially situated use of writing that I described in the previous chapters, I examine the next stage of inkshedding—the reading and marking of the text in which the writing becomes public, and in which the imagined reader is real.

The set-up of the conference room facilitated public reading of inkshedding texts. At the conference, typically groups of about eight people sat at round tables. Depending on the size of the conference, anywhere from five to ten tables filled the conference room (though each table was not always full). When the writers at each table finished writing their texts, they put them in the centre of the table and took one another's texts to read. As individuals read the texts, they drew lines in the margins, bracketed, or otherwise highlighted whatever parts of the texts stood out to them as significant. Some people even wrote the occasional comment in the margin as a response to what they had read, so that the text became a kind of written conversation. The process was repeated with as many of the texts as time permitted. Sometimes, if time allowed, groups at different tables exchanged their inkshedding piles in an effort to get more circulation. Alternately, when seating arrangements were not conducive to small-group seating, inkshed texts were taped to the walls and participants walked around the room in order to read what had been written.

Inkshedders argued that one benefit of this public reading was that it gave all participants an equal chance to express themselves and be heard. The reading stage in inkshedding allowed time for individual voices to be heard. In this chapter I critically examine the perspective of equality as I look at how people read and annotated texts, and how this reading contributed to membership in the collective. The texts that I use to approach this discussion include not just the tangible pen on paper texts created in the process of inkshedding, but also the human texts that were read and circulated through participation in the conference.

Like words on a page passed from one reader to the next, participants at an Inkshed conference were written texts, influenced by the values, ideas, and experiences they encountered. An individual arrived at a conference as a text in progress, a text already written upon by prior life experience. Just as the inkshedding text was circulated and marked by readers, the human text was circulated through discussions, presentations, and other forms of participation. And like the inkshedding text, as other inkshedders read the human text, they left their mark, highlighting valuable sections, thus altering the text. While individual agency helped determine who would touch it, the human text was shaped and transformed by the social interactions that it encountered. Human texts were marked by the events of their lives. They arrived at Inkshed conferences already written and marked upon, to be read and marked again.

Texts, as Bakhtin (1986) explained, are socially situated and are the culmination of a myriad of background experiences. He wrote:

> Any speaker is himself a respondent to a greater or lesser degree. He is not, after all, the first speaker, the one who disturbs the eternal silence of the universe. And he presupposes not only the existence of the language system he is using, but also the existence of preceding utterances—his own and others'—with which his given utterance enters into one kind of relation or another . . . . Any utterance is a link in a very complexly organized chain of other utterances. (p. 69)

Like print or visual texts, humans are also socially situated and enter any conversation as a product of past experiences, ready to take on parts of new conversations. They are, like Bakhtin's "utterance," imbued with meaning, depth, and complexity as a result of previous and current experiences. This chapter explores the literacy practice that is the circulation, reading and marking of both print and human texts as part of the Inkshed experience and as a way of understanding the trajectory from peripheral to full participation.

To begin my discussion of reading and circulation of human and paper texts, I present two short vignettes that illustrate some of the ways that inkshedding equalizes. Although neither of these two vignettes describes the reading process in the actual inkshedding activity, they speak to the ways that individuals and their opinions were valued and were given voice in conference settings. They reflect the fundamental values behind reading in inkshedding. I follow these vignettes with a discussion of the theoretical perspective explaining why inkshedding has the potential to equalize, and the ways that it does so with both written and human texts. However, my data suggest (as implied by the intensity of the feelings of vulnerability described in the previous chapter) that to assume that inkshedding is an activity in which everyone felt equal is not reflective of many people's experiences. The next two short vignettes illustrate the suggestion that not all inkshedding was equally valued. The first illustrates the way in which I was marked as a text at the first Inkshed conference I attended. The second describes one way that texts were read. I use these vignettes to launch a discussion of how inkshedding marginalized some groups of people and favoured others. This, I argue, impacted the opportunities that participants had to participate in meaningful and legitimate ways, and therefore, membership in the collective. However, it should be noted that because I am primarily interested in the ways that inkshedding facilitates membership, my data are not sufficient to examine extensively the more negative side of inkshedding. I touch on things that may detract from membership, but do not dwell on them in detail. I do so with an awareness that I am presenting only one of many possible perspectives.

Vignette 1

CATTW [Canadian Association of Teachers of Technical Writing now known as the Canadian Association for the Study of Discourse and Writing (CASDW)] *2006—the conference room is full to overflowing. Latecomers sit on the stairs that lead to the centre of the room where Ken Hyland has just finished his keynote presentation. Intellectual enthusiasm and energy permeate the room. Even I feel caught up by the research he has presented. Many hands are in the air as people wait their turn to ask questions and make comments. A woman below me and to my left is drawing parallels between Hyland's work and someone else's. Someone behind me asks a question about methods. Someone across the room asks questions about implications. The moderator of the session tries to make sure the less vocal people in the room have the opportunity to speak and tries to cut off the questions to keep the session within its time frame. I find myself wishing for a way to expand on some of my own thoughts but realize that, with the lack of time and intimidating audience, I will keep my mouth shut. We need a forum, I think to myself, where everyone can participate in this discussion. It doesn't work when only one person can have the floor at once. And suddenly, I finally make the connection. Inkshedding isn't an activity designed to make people feel uncomfortable (although that may be what happens). It's designed for situations exactly like this, where so many people do have something to say, where people want to pursue and explore ideas together. I finally understand it is a way of letting everyone speak. I find myself a little sad that CATTW doesn't inkshed.*

Vignette 2

Inkshed XX Friday morning, I momentarily indulge in the decadence of being alone—no children jumping on my bed, no one demanding breakfast. I languish for a moment, but all too soon, the familiar anxiety of yesterday returns. I am excited to see what the day will offer, but still worry about fitting in. A quick shower, some clean clothes, and I am ready to face the dining room for breakfast. I wonder who will be there. Will I know anyone? Who will I sit with? What will I talk about? The halls are empty as I emerge from my room. I surmise that breakfast, or at least a leisurely breakfast, is not a priority for most Inkshedders who I imagine still clinging to their last vestiges of sleep for the day. Somewhere ahead of me I hear a solitary door open and close. I make my way to the outer door of the complex that will take me to the road to the main building where the dining room and conference room are both housed. It's a gray looking morning, and I pull on my sweater before stepping out the door. As I round the edge of the parking lot I see someone already out ahead of me. She is halfway down the hill. Far enough away, I assume, that we don't need to worry about morning small talk. But as she hears my footsteps behind her, she glances back. I see it is Margaret Procter, one of the conference organizers. Rather than continuing on, she stops, and waits for me to catch up. I am pleasantly surprised by this display of amity from such a busy and important woman. I quicken my pace so she doesn't have too long to wait. Later that morning when she begins the session, she does so with the proclamation that, "we need to do lots of inkshedding so Miriam can see how it's done."

Equality

The Written Text

One of the things that Inkshedders celebrated about inkshedding was the way that it equalized participants. Regardless of educational background or affiliation, everyone was given the opportunity to share thoughts and contribute to an ongoing discussion. Anthony Paré, in many mentoring discussions with me, described how, in academia, students are typically relegated to eavesdropping on the proverbial Burkean conversation (Burke, 1941). While the learned knowledge makers (well-established figures in the discipline) engage in debates, negotiations, and otherwise construct knowledge, newcomers to academia (undergraduate students) listen in at the parlour door and attempt to summarize and draw connections among the most significant voices. When the newcomers become graduate students, the door is thrown open and they are suddenly expected, through the negotiation of a supervisor, to participate in the parlour conversation. This metaphor helps to describe the positions and directions of power typical in academia. However, what inkshedding did at the conferences was to allow everyone who participated the same opportunity to be heard. It allowed everyone to take part in the conversation regardless of power differentials that may have existed such as professional status, institutional affiliation, or publication record. This was because no single voice was allowed to dominate. While an ordinary conversation, such as the exchange I described at CATTW, allows only one voice to speak at a time (and then, the more self-assured and articulate ones), in inkshedding, everyone could "speak." In other words, everyone contributed to the broader conversation through their writing—it was not the loudest or most aggressive people who took over the conversation because that opportunity did not exist. Everyone wrote and everyone circulated what they had written before any oral voices took over or monopolized the discussion. This opportunity for self-expression was seen as positive and valuable. As one long-time Inkshedder explained:

> I am just so glad . . . that we have a chance to respond to ideas not orally because I find that's sometimes more difficult to do than doing it on a blank page. Standing up, or speaking, or getting my words in—some people have no trouble, that's to me why inkshedding is so valuable. It's the one place where you can do that stuff. (Focus group interview, 5/13/2005)

As this excerpt illustrates, not everyone felt comfortable speaking out loud. Oral conversations tend to favor dominant and articulate personality types. Through inkshedding, however, it was possible to join a conversation without fighting to be heard over the experts or highly verbal people because all voice went on paper to be circulated for others to read.

Russ Hunt (2004), in an article originally presented at Inkshed XVI, explained how, in the creation of inkshedding, he and Jim Reither tried to create something that promoted participation and dialogue. He explained how, in his opinion, the writing activity facilitated a democratic process, or a process in which everyone had equal opportunity to be heard:

> It's also important that during inkshedding ideas, positions, and questions which would not otherwise attain a hearing have a better opportunity to get "on the floor" than they would in an oral discussion. A

significant force in the original impetus for using inkshedding in classrooms was the perception that classroom discussions tend to be dominated by a few voices. This is natural, as the "bandwidth" for classroom discussion—at least for *whole* [emphasis his] class discussions—is very narrow. Only one voice can be heard at any one time: for what *everyone* [emphasis his] thought about an event to be articulated and discussed is not only practically difficult, even in a small class, but socially constraining: the first few utterances tend very strongly to determine and focus the range of discussion, and effectively determine the kinds of questions or issues which will be raised. Anthony Paré, in a comment on an earlier draft of this piece, says, "I've always felt that inkshedding allowed for the individual exploration of a top-of-the-head response before that response is deflected, diminished, or destroyed by the first question or comment spoken out loud. Inkshedding allows each member of the group to 'gather' her/his thoughts before they are scattered by that first, articulate, confident person who gets up to say what you weren't even thinking about."

In this excerpt, Hunt articulated the dichotomy between a traditional one-voice-at-a-time conversation, and an Inkshed conversation in which everyone participates at once. He pointed out the value of letting participants express themselves before they could be influenced by others' ideas. Thus, through inkshedding, participants had the opportunity to express their initial thoughts and ideas before they could be hijacked and carried away with the dominant voice.

One of the benefits of this general participation was the multiplicity of perspectives that it provided. By encouraging many voices to participate at once, inkshedding offered a dynamic interchange. This variety of viewpoints and ideas provided more depth than might have been had in a traditional conversation in which one idea was expressed at a time. A comment by Rick Coe, an original Inkshedder, supports this idea, and explains the value of multiple interactions:

> The best thing about this, as distinguished from what normally happens, is that you get to hear all these people who you wouldn't get to hear. And it turns out that lots of them are thinking really interesting and insightful things. And that happens here, and it doesn't happen at oral discussions. (Focus group interview, 5/13/2005)

In other words, inkshedding provided a forum in which otherwise quiet voices could be heard. The variety of these voices provided interesting and valuable contributions. The vignette I used earlier describing CATTW illustrates Coe's point of view. Many perspectives went unheard because of the constraints of oral discourse. Thus, by using writing as a medium for discussion, more voices and therefore more ideas came forward during the reading stage. More opportunity was given for meaningful participation leading to fuller participation in general. This, in turn, provided for a rich exchange and dialogue because the conversation was not limited to those who were loudest. Instead, the community engaged together, thus strengthening membership.

The Human Text

Valuing multiple voices and opportunities for meaningful participation characterizes both the inkshedding activity and the community that used it. For this reason, many people talk not just about inkshedding as a democratizing activity in which everyone participates, but about Inkshed as a community that equalized. The Inkshedder attitude was that everyone had something valuable to contribute. Despite diverse backgrounds, everyone, from expert scholars in the field to graduate students just beginning their careers, was welcomed into the collective and no hierarchy was encouraged. One Inkshedder explained how the inkshedding activity was a reflection of how people were accepted at the conferences. He said:

> We think, it seems to me, that we have agreed in many ways that we're all equal here. I mean, that we all have an equal contribution to make. I mean, I think one thing that's nice about inkshedding . . . is that it gives people voice. And so we can kind of democratize activity because everybody has a chance to speak. Whereas in table or even large group sessions, people, I mean, those of us who are, you know, vocal and the most aggressive, have a tendency to take over those conversations. (Focus group interview, 5/13/2005)

In other words, like the inkshedding activity, all participants in the community had the chance to participate without worrying about pre-existing social hierarchies. This kind of equalizing was purposeful and conscientious and existed because of the nature of the community. The community valued dialogic interaction and collaboration. Thus, in the same way that everyone's voice was valued in the activity, many Inkshedders worked hard to make sure this same equality existed in the community at large. Just as a written text circulated so everyone read it, individuals were like texts as they circulated through the community and there was considerable effort to ensure that participants had a wide circulation and reading.

The vignette in which I noted how Margaret Procter waited for me describes one of the ways that I was made to feel part of the community. Margaret, a busy conference organizer, could easily have continued on her way ahead of me without needing to make excuses. Instead, she chose to wait for me. She knew I was just a graduate student, and not even contributing in the form of a presentation to the conference, and yet, she waited and then walked and talked with me. Margaret did not "read" me as just another graduate student unworthy of her time. On the contrary, she seemed sincerely interested in what I had to say. She treated me as an equal.

Like Margaret, most Inkshedders made a conscious effort to make people feel comfortable and equal in the community. They made an effort to "sign onto that collaborative medial [communicative] social model" (Nan Johnson, focus group interview, 5/13/2005)—that is, a collective effort to mutually and equally engage—and learn from each other. One of the ways that this kind of collaboration was both facilitated and encouraged was through the isolated settings of the conferences. Participants were always together—at single-session presentations, at meals, at talent night, and during unstructured social time. Through this constant interaction every opportunity was given for people to circulate, read others, and be read. Anthony Paré once pointed out that it was possible to go to other conferences and never know the name of the person sitting beside you. At Inkshed, this did not happen. Instead, multiple opportunities existed to read other texts, and to be read by others. The wider the circulation, in general, the more individuals came to feel part of the collective.

Many original and long-time Inkshedders purposefully tried to facilitate newcomer circulation. They made a special effort to read, or interact with, as many people as they could during the conference so that newcomers felt validated, important, and like they had something valuable to contribute (this touches on "highlighting," in which certain parts of the text stand out as worthwhile or resonant, which I discuss in more detail in the next section). One Inkshedder who made an extra effort to read as many texts (i.e., people) as she could and was particularly influential in my circulation in the Inkshed community was Kenna Manos. At my first conference, she surprised me by inviting me for a walk in the woods with herself and another long-time Inkshedder. I suspected they were planning their talent night act, and, fearful of being roped in, declined the invitation. The genuineness of the offer struck me, however, and somehow that simple acknowledgment of my presence helped me feel "highlighted," in resonance with the collective. At subsequent conferences Kenna always engaged with me as a long-time trusted colleague. Every time I attended a conference with her, I was struck by the way she appeared to have a genuine interest in everyone there, and mingled with as many people as she could. Kenna summarized her drive to be inclusive. She explained: "We want them [newcomers] to become part of the culture, to feel comfortable in the culture" (Focus group interview, 5/13/2005). Inkshedders wanted newcomers to feel like they could participate, like they were valued, and like they were part of the collective. This effort at inclusion, by Kenna and Margaret and many others, contributed to a culture of equality where newcomers and old-timers alike were invited to participate. The result of this inclusivity and sense of equality was that like the inkshedding texts, human texts got a wide distribution and circulation. Through the set-up of the conference, people had multiple opportunities to mingle and put names to faces, but also to interact in more meaningful ways. Conversations were carried from conference tables to lunch tables. Connections were made in the evening over drinks in the bar. Talent night stripped away pride and showed not just a goofy side of Inkshedders, but also, sometimes, a deeper and more personal part of a person's being—like the woman who shared a short story she had written that detailed some of her childhood experiences coming to grips with religion, or the woman who spoke of her mother's death. Each of these opportunities for contact or interaction provided opportunity for a text to be read, to be marked by the interaction with the reader, and to leave a mark in return. Individuals both read and were read and thus they participated in meaningful ways in the community.

This participation led to a feeling of engagement and therefore membership in the collective. Comments by newcomers reflect the impact of this inclusive effort. One person, describing their first time at Inkshed, wrote: "I attend my first Inkshed and immediately feel the support of a national community" (The Wall, Inkshed XX, 2003). Another wrote: "I land in Nfld not knowing a soul; I leave a member of a community that extends to this day" (The Wall, Inkshed XX, 2003). Although not universal, these excerpts echo my own experience of inclusion, welcome and participation in Inkshed. Thus, in the same way the activity sought to equalize participation, the Inkshed community valued participation and tried to help everyone feel comfortable and part of the collective. Efforts to value all participants often resulted in newcomers being able to gain confidence participating in the community and thus feel that they were community members. This perspective of Inkshed serves to illustrate Wenger's description of a CoP. Because power structures and hierarchies do not appear in Wenger's description, this very positive perspective of the Inkshed community serves to show how a CoP might function if no power differentials existed.

However, in spite of efforts by the community to make everyone feel welcome and included, not everyone did. In the same way that some written texts resonate well and stand out to the reader, some individuals stood out as well. Like mine, their experiences tended to be positive and inclusive, while others, whether through their writing or other interactions, were left feeling marginalized. In discussing LPP Lave & Wenger (1991) suggested that newcomers should learn to participate in similar ways. That is, given consistent circumstances in which to participate, newcomers will learn the same way. The learning experience or participation will not vary. However, this tenet of LPP appears problematic. In the same way that newcomers dealt with feelings of anxiety in different ways (as discussed in the previous chapter), individual attitudes, beliefs, and values impacted the ways that individuals participated. As a result, newcomers had a variety of responses to the Inkshed experience. Some connected and thrived the way I did. Others felt left out, marginalized, isolated, and even resentful. The following vignettes describe the way that my personal characteristics influenced both who read me and how I was read. Highlighting parts of Miriam as a text ensured a wider reading, circulation and therefore participation in the community for me. I relate these vignettes because they are easily accessible; others were more reticent to divulge their stories in this form. However, by including these vignettes, I am not implying that everyone received such positive interactions. Rather, I share them in order to highlight that my case was exceptional and that few people got the same reception I did.

Vignette 3

Thursday Evening, Inkshed XX. As I sit on the deck with the other Inkshedders feeling awkward because I don't know anyone here, I see Ann Beer arrive. I am surprised to see her, but happy to see a familiar face. Ann is one of my professors at McGill who has shown enthusiasm for a research project on inkshedding. I see her greet a few people as she comes in. She spots me as she is in mid-embrace with Kenna Manos.

"Kenna," she says turning Kenna toward me, "have you met Miriam yet? She's doing her PhD on inkshedding—with Anthony."

"Really?" says Kenna. "Are you here to spy on us?"

"Oh, no, no," I quickly respond, "nothing like that."

"Well, let me know if I can help at all. I've been here since the beginning and I'd be happy to talk with you."

"Thanks," I answer, "that's great, I'll keep it in mind."

And then Kenna and Ann are swept away in catching up and talking with others.

I next encounter Ann in the dining room as I am heading for a table with my loaded plate of food. She seems engaged in conversations between two tables. As I pass she says, "Oh, Miriam, have you met Russ yet?" And turning to Russ at the table behind her she says, "Russ, this is Miriam, she's doing her PhD on inkshedding. With Anthony. Isn't that marvelous!"

"Yes," answers Russ, "I'm really looking forward to it."

And so she continues. The following morning she introduces me to Nan Johnson. During the coffee break she announces me to Sharron Wall. And by lunch time it seems that everyone knows that I am doing a PhD on inkshedding, with Anthony.

Vignette 4

Friday morning, Inkshed XXII. I am one of the first ones into the conference room after breakfast. I position myself at a table in the middle of the back of the room and glance over the schedule for the morning. I am happy to see that more than just recognizing some of the names on the schedule, I have memories and connections with many of them as well. I see that Brock and Barbara are starting off the morning and I smile knowing that it is bound to be an interesting presentation.

I find myself thinking back to my first Inkshed conference and how uncomfortable I was. The contrast is drastic. I know people now; I have developed relationships with them. I am surprised at how happy I am to be here. The academic year has not gone well. I am frustrated and ready to give up on school altogether—too many conflicting demands on my time and I don't seem to be getting anywhere with research. I promised myself I would at least attend one more conference (this one) before I give it up. I have to give it one more chance.

Sharron Wall comes into the room and comes to sit with me. We haven't had a chance to visit yet. We are both at McGill, but I think I see more of her at conferences than I do in Montreal. I know her enough to have a polite conversation, but not much more than that. We chat, and then comes the inevitable question, "How's the research?" I am evasive in my answer. I am trying to prepare my comprehensive exams, but . . . . Sharron probes. She asks pointed questions, and soon, as the room is filling up around us, I find myself venting all my recent frustrations. At some point Nan Johnson joins our table and Sharron brings her into the discussion. I am surprised by the intensity of their support, by their frankness, and by their understanding.

Eventually, the room is full and the first session starts, but I am distracted by our conversation and it stays hovering and replaying in my head for the rest of the conference.

It doesn't take long before we arrive at the inevitable inkshedding. It doesn't bother me today. I've been paying enough attention to the speakers—listening for the thought that strikes me; the thought that I can expand on in my inkshedding. We are given leave to begin writing and so I do. The activity goes quickly. I add my paper to the growing pile in the middle of the table and pull out another one to read.

Beside me, I see that Sharron is reading mine. I find myself aware of this, but not too bothered. I've just finished pouring my heart out about my PhD woes and had nothing but support. It's okay if Sharron reads the thoughts inspired by the presentation—even if there's nothing to them. "Whose is this?" she asks.

"Mine," I tell her. "What's wrong, can't you read my writing?"

"Oh, it's yours!" she says. "Well, now that I know it's yours, I'm going to go back and read it again."

"What, are you giving me special treatment or something?"

"Well, I want to know what you have to say."

"Wait a minute! You mean it makes a difference to you who wrote it?" I ask, intrigued that an inkshed could be valued not just for what it said, but for who said it.

"Of course," she answers.

"Well, give that here then," I say as I take the page from her. I sign my name at the bottom of the page, and never write an anonymous inkshed again.

Highlighting

In the second stage of inkshedding, not only are texts circulated and read, but they are also marked, highlighting the ways in which they resonate with the reader, or the way the reader has become mutually engaged with the writer. The two vignettes I have just shared reflect a fundamental problem with the notion of equality in Inkshed and in inkshedding: despite efforts to the contrary, some inkshedding was more valued than others. Texts, human or written, were not all read in the same way. In the case of my first Inkshed conference, it was as if every time Ann introduced me to someone and said I was studying inkshedding with Anthony, she was highlighting a particular part of the text of Miriam. Inkshedders suggested that when they read the inkshedding texts, they looked for something they thought would resonate with other Inkshedders that would be meaningful to them, and mark the text accordingly. In describing how he read and marked an inkshedding text, Rick Coe explained:

> There's something in that and you say other people
> would find this interesting or find this funny or useful
> or insightful . . . . I'm saying this thing is something that
> should go to the group because it will have some value,
> in my opinion. (Focus group interview, 5/13/2005)

In other words, when something resonated and he thought it would also resonate with the group, he marked it up to call attention to it for the next reader and as something worth engagement. Another Inkshedder explained:

> I would hope that what those publications do . . .
> should continue the conversation. I mean there are
> certainly inksheds that don't invite you to continue
> the conversation, and there are things that do. And I
> have a tendency to mark those things that I think will
> be provocative, and will provoke people to think more
> about it. (Focus group interview, 5/13/2005)

Like Rick Coe, this reader highlighted texts that had some kind of engagement with others.

The way that Ann Beer introduced me to other Inkshedders highlighted me in the same way that these Inkshedders described highlighting an inkshedding text. She noted something she thought was valuable to the community and would inspire conversation—not only that I was studying inkshedding, but that I was doing it under the supervision of long-time and well-respected Inkshedder Anthony Paré. She highlighted the things about me that would resonate with the collective. In the years since that initial experience I learned to connect in other meaningful ways with the community (as I discuss in more detail in the following chapter.) However, that initial experience highlighted important things that would grab the attention of the collective immediately. As a result, Ann's enthusiastic introductions ensured a wide circulation and interaction for Miriam the text.

My experience at my first Inkshed conference differed from the experience of a first-time Inkshedder a few years earlier. Instead of my experience in which I felt widely circulated, he shared how his personal text was virtually ignored. He wrote:

> The conference began on the first evening with a large circle in which people went around and stated, "My first Inkshed . . ." and recounted tales of the previous Inkshed conferences and their favourite memories. For those of us there for the first time (and we made up perhaps 20% of the group) that was very, very excluding. (Personal communication, 6/10/2007)

This example points to the ways that some human texts were valued over others. This participant described one way in which veteran Inkshedders were valued over newcomers and the subsequent feelings of marginalization that ensued.

The vignette in which Sharron read my text more carefully once she knew it was mine shows how important readings of human texts were to the inkshedding activity. In the previous example, the writer did not have an opportunity to be read, and as a result of this and other experiences which left him feeling marginalized, did not return to Inkshed. However, the other Inkshedders present in his account were given opportunity to strengthen their existing relationships through their memories. Like my experience with Sharron, this kind of emphasis on relationships may have contributed to the way the conference emerged where (as I described in the previous section) participants were given multiple opportunities to interact and engage. Sharron took the time to read me and know me before ever reading my written text. Had she not, she would have quickly dismissed my messy handwriting as not worth the effort to decipher (something she was about to do, but chose to ask for clarification instead). Unfortunately, the participant who felt marginalized while others shared their memories did not have a chance to be read and thus did not share the same feelings of value that I experienced.

Other Inkshedders admitted to the importance of knowing who you were reading. In one of many conversations I had with him, Russ Hunt admitted that he sometimes moved from table to table during the reading stage because he wanted to know what particular people had written (Field notes, 5/13/2005). Similarly, Tania Smith (2000) in an ethnographic study of Inkshed, noted that because many Inkshedders had been working together for many years and knew each other very well, they valued what each other had to say. As a result, they searched for specific texts in order to know what certain people had to say on a topic. Tania quoted one of the participants of her study who said:

Overall, the process seems quite interesting but not all VOICES or INKSHEDS are heard . . . there is a certain problem with that . . . for example, my INKSHEDS were never selected and often, they were not read on the table . . . where I was sitting. Quite often, more experienced INKSHEDDERS read the writings of their peers and not of newcomers like myself. Also, my comments probably did not correspond to the majority's cultural viewpoint so I did not benefit from feedback such as "I think the same way" or "similar to the point I made" . . . rather, my comments were for the most part never read or commented on by my peers . . . . I think the process of INKSHEDDING is quite interesting but perhaps the issue of EQUITY needs to be addressed to ensure that more VOICES are heard and picked up and that newcomers are also read and commented etc.

As this example illustrates, despite the fact that extra attention given to me worked positively in my case, the converse also happened, and a conundrum like the one I raised in the previous chapter was reinforced. That is, it was difficult to participate without knowing the audience or being known, but it was equally challenging to know the audience, or become known without participating. As some of the foregoing examples suggest, things happened that left individuals feeling marginalized and outside the general reading in the community instead of feeling valued for their personal or written texts.

Marginalization

Notwithstanding the efforts of many Inkshedders and the intended values of inclusivity and equality in inkshedding, individuals will always respond in individual ways. In the same way that I responded positively to the Inkshed setting, others did not, nor did all others share my positive welcome. I connected to the values, beliefs and practices of the community because the community opened to me. Others, however, remained on the periphery for too long and therefore did not share in the ideals of Inkshed togetherness. Some found the community too self-promoting and weak in theory (Personal communication, 12/15/2006) to the point that they even found it boring (Personal communication, 12/14/2006). Thus, despite sometimes great efforts, and sometimes not so great efforts of the community to ensure that everyone felt welcome, or equal, individuals reacted differently. And despite an effort to "check baggage" and other identities at the door (a metaphor generated by a focus group discussion used to refer to the way that everyone shares common interests and is equal when at the conference, 5/13/2005), participants remained individuals and as such reacted differently to situations as they occurred. As a result, some individuals felt marginalized. These feelings existed with (but were not limited to) individuals as texts as well as written texts as a result of background experiences and writing styles.

Background Experiences

In the previous chapter, I described how Russ Hunt saw the multidisciplinary nature of the community as positive. He felt that it brought richness to the community. However, this multidisciplinarity was also cause for at least one person to feel marginalized. One person who was less involved in academic discussions of writing described his feelings in the following way:

> I have always felt a bit of an outsider at Inkshed conferences. Simply because all other members are academically affiliated and I don't share all of their concerns. I feel welcome and comfortable, but a wee bit alien—sometimes as if I'm an emblem of writing in the workplace, an emblem of "otherness." Thus I feel a member of a community I very much value, but there resides a little frisson of being different, being half a step "outside." (Inkshedding text, 5/9/2004)

Thus, despite feeling welcome, this writer felt marginal because he did not take part in the same academic discourses as other Inkshedders.

Another source of marginalization came in the form of nationality. One of the people I met my first year at Inkshed was also there for her first time. She was an American living and teaching in Canada. When I encountered her a few years later at another conference, she swore she would never go back to Inkshed. She felt the community was unfriendly and unwelcoming, and, most insulting, had sung anti-war songs during the talent night in response to George W. Bush's decision to go to war in Iraq. She explained that because she was American, she felt like the whole room had been singing against her and was furious that politics would have any place at an academic conference. She also felt that Canadians in general were much less friendly and supportive than their American counterparts. She described the difference between CATTW (now CASDW) and ATTW

(Association of Teachers of Technical Writing), for example, as night and day—relating far more positively to the American conference (Personal communication, 5/27/2006). Because Inkshedders valued discussions of their teaching and research in Canadian settings, it is not surprising that some people working in other countries may have felt marginalized.

Ideological discrepancies also existed. One Canadian researcher, who focused on the exploration of theoretical perspectives, told me that she found the conference too introspective and self-indulgent. Although she valued some of the things that the community had to offer (like the listserv and Inkshed publications), she preferred to attend CATTW, which she felt was more research-oriented (Field notes, 5/27/2006). Similarly, another participant explained that although he valued the listserv community for the information it provided, he was unimpressed with the conferences. Like the woman who found Inkshed too inwardly focused, this participant found the conference weak on theory and too introspective. He also preferred to attend CATTW conferences.

These three areas of background experience illustrate the ways in which people may have found it difficult to participate or may have chosen not to participate in the conferences. Consequently, full participation became a challenge at best.

Style

In terms of the actual inkshedding activity itself, certain aspects of the process may have privileged some and marginalized others, such as the ability to write quickly and effectively on the spot. While some did this easily, others did not. They required time to think and revise. Anthony Paré described this in the following way:

There are people who have a real facility. They have a flair. They have a nice turn of phrase, quickly. Not everybody does. And that's the French expression *pensées d'escalier* [thoughts on the stairs], the thoughts you have after you have left whatever situation you were in. And I think, "I should have said . . . Oh! Oh! And I should have said that." Well, I have those all the time. I sit through situations in which I am struck dumb, and then afterwards I think, "Why didn't I say blah, blah, blah?" It was the right thing to say. Somebody should have said it, but no one did. It was so obvious, but I didn't think about it at that time. And I think that is true. I think that inkshedding favours a particular kind of thinker, not necessarily the best kind of thinker, but someone who comes up with quick thoughts and responses. It doesn't leave room for much reflection. (Personal interview, 12/5/2006)

While some people can think and write quickly on the spot and can come up with something that sounds intelligent and articulate, others have a harder time with the immediacy of the response and, only once the moment has passed, think of the clever and appropriate words that might have resonated with others. Without that quick facility for words, participants struggle, feel awkward and vulnerable.

Thus, the inkshedding process privileges those writers who are quick thinking, non-planning, and non-revising. Russ Hunt explored this issue with another Inkshedder. They explained this privilege in the following way:

> Terry [pseudonym]: So in a sense, you're still privileging
> the people who can think faster . . . and articulate
> faster.
>
> Russ: But it privileges a different cut . . . it privileges
> a different slice of the population than a normal
> conference format . . . . (Focus group interview,
> 5/13/2005)

This sort of privileging created a distinct disadvantage for those who could not think quickly or write quickly, a disadvantage that may have affected some individuals' abilities to participate in the activity and therefore led to feelings of marginalization. Because of their predisposition, they were never truly in a position to participate equally. For example, an original Inkshedder explained that because he was unable to write quickly and effectively, many years went by before any of his inkshedding was "published." He explained: "It damages the writer who is an inveterate planner, and you know . . . for ten, twelve years, I never got anything published" (Focus group interview, 5/13/2005).

This same kind of privilege seems to have affected not just the written text, but the human text as well. Those who did not take risks by joining in dinner conversations or making an effort to meet new people, or were not "allowed" to take risks because activities were exclusive to those who had participated in previous conferences, did not have the same kind of experience as those who were confident, socialized easily, or, like myself, were given quick entrance to the community. While some people found Inkshed friendly and welcoming, others found it insular and difficult to take part in. One person compared going to an Inkshed conference to being invited into someone's living room and then being ignored. Another person said: "The attitudes of "veteran" Inkshedders toward younger scholars were dismissive and cliquish" (Personal communication, 6/8/2007). He continued describing his problem with the Inkshed community by writing: "I think that there is a terrible cliquishness about Inkshed that stems from a kind of moral superiority about particular practices" (Personal communication, 6/8/2007). He went on to express that at least three other scholars had the same kinds of feelings that he did and cut themselves off from Inkshed, thus pointing to the role of privilege in membership. Others articulated their experiences in other ways. Consider, for example, the experience that one individual had when she attended the conference for the first time. Like the other examples, her experience describes a feeling of having not been appropriately circulated or read as a text. She wrote:

> I don't feel like I've become a member of the Inkshed community yet—for two reasons. 1) This is my first Inkshed conference and 2) the opportunity for discussion never came. Hence, I don't feel like I've gotten to know the whole group or it me. (Inkshedding text, 5/9/2004)

Her perception that "the opportunity for discussion never came" is revealing of the kind of experience she had, and, like so many other aspects of Inkshed and inkshedding that I have pointed out, suggests a predisposition to participation in the community. Whether the collective never provided opportunities for engagement, or the writer did not engage in the opportunities, or both, this writer did not circulate her text in the ongoing dialogue. This excerpt, along with the previous ones, highlights the different kinds of experiences that people had. While I was able to find many opportunities for discussion, this individual was unable to find those opportunities to connect with others, whether to read and highlight others or to be read and highlighted herself. The variance between my own experience and others' seems to reflect Bourdieu's (1977) notions of social and cultural capital as a way of explaining differences in experiences. In other words, background is one way of accounting for the diverse ways that people experienced inkshedding as well as the ways that Inkshedders experienced new members.

Another way that texts appeared to be marginalized and thus unequal in the inkshedding process was through handwriting. Quite simply, neat handwriting was privileged over messy handwriting. In other words, handwriting that was neat and easy to read was more likely to be read, and therefore be marked and even published. Like speech in an accent too thick to be understood, poor handwriting was passed over in favour of that which was quick and easy to read in a short time period—regardless of who had written it. During a conference presentation at Kamloops, I led a discussion about how people felt like members of the community. The issue of being "published" was raised. One woman complained that she did not write the "right" things and was therefore never published. In response, another woman, a long time member of the community, disclosed that in her whole Inkshed career she had been "published" less than five times. The explanation was that her handwriting, which was agreed by the community to be virtually illegible, made her inkshedding far too difficult to read even though she had valuable things to say. In my own experience, if the handwriting was difficult to read, I tended to skim over it very quickly and not give it the time and attention that it may have deserved.

Thus, although many aspects of Inkshed and inkshedding did equalize and democratize, many people found it difficult to find opportunities to engage, and, as a result, felt marginalized. The converse was also true. Some were able to engage more than others (as I was because of Ann's highlighting) and therefore were able to move to a position of full participation.

Summary

Both the inkshedding activity and the Inkshed community (particularly through the conference) facilitated a kind of democratic or equal interaction. This was a result of the way that texts, both human and written, were circulated. In theory, everyone had equal opportunity to express themselves and be heard. The reality, however, was somewhat different. Some texts may have received more or less attention depending on their authors, the relationships already there, or the perceived contributions. Although some people and texts were favoured in a positive way through circulation and participation, others were not. Those who were unable to find themselves in a position in which they felt equal or like they belonged in the community often never came back to the conference. However, some, who shared inkshedding values, managed to throw themselves into the process for circulation (both figuratively and literally), and managed to find a place of belonging and contribute to the membership.

As my experiences and those of others illustrate, social dynamics and hierarchies (formal or perceived) impact the ways in which people are able to engage. In addition, the individuality that people have may also impact the kind of experience they have within a CoP. In a broader academic context, this helps to explain the variety of experiences that students may have even within the same class. It also points to the challenge of teaching such a variety of individuals.

5

Full Participation: A Public Presence

In the previous chapters, I described the values characteristic of the Inkshed community and the inkshedding activity in an effort to explain the ways that writing practices contribute to or detract from membership. I described the process of membership, or the process of becoming an Inkshedder, by examining the stages of inkshedding for both the literal writing process and as a way of understanding human dynamics at conferences. In this chapter I describe the final stage of inkshedding—publication—and look at the published texts both as a tool for and a symbol of membership.

At Inkshed conferences the publication stage worked something like this: after the inkshedding texts circulated as much as time allowed, they were whisked away to another room where there was a computer and a printer. Each set of conference organizers managed this stage slightly differently. Sometimes, Inkshedders volunteered or were recruited to edit, that is, to select passages to be typed up and then to type them. Other times, graduate students were hired to key in the highlighted sections. At one conference I attended, a secretary (whom I never actually saw) came with the conference organizers and spent the entire conference secluded in a room typing up highlighted inkshed texts so that we had them within an hour or two of the presentations (Field notes, 5/9/2006). Sometimes difficulties arose in preparing highlighted sections of texts for publication because meaningful passages were not clearly marked. In one difficult case, the graduate students assigned to process the texts printed off inkshedding excerpts that began or ended midsentence. Since the original texts were highlighted with lines in the margins, linguistic boundaries had not been delineated. The students assigned to edit and type had not attended the conference sessions in question, and the texts were decontextualized for them. Thus they were unable to make meaningful editorial interpretations or judgments about excerpts. Consequently, instructions came back to Inkshedders to clarify what they marked (Field notes, 5/8/2004). Some years, when the typists were Inkshedders, they acted as an editorial board. Early in the conference, when they were still energetic, anything with two or more lines got published. Later as energy waned, only sections with three or four lines were typed up. Sometimes, if passages from two texts were similar, only one of them would be typed up (Focus group interview, 5/13/2005).

Once the highlighted texts were typed up, they were photocopied and distributed to conference members. The purpose of this stage was to reinsert significant ideas back into the ongoing dialogue during the conference. Because the texts were edited and typed by a separate body and then distributed to the public, as happens with academic publications, I call this stage publication.

Although this chapter explores the literal process of publication as I have described above, it also looks at the public aspect of publication.

That is, the root word for publication is public. For my purposes here, I describe publication as making a text public. While I focus primarily on inkshedding texts being made public and the ramifications of that, I also look at the human text and the making public of that human text. I describe the human text as an individual, but also apply the role of the text to the Inkshed community. Like an inkshedding text or a human text participating in Inkshed, the Inkshed collective has a public face in the broader discipline of Canadian writing studies. Hence, when I talk about movement to a public place, or about a text being public, I use it to refer to the ways that single entities (a written text, an individual, or a community) are exposed to and interact with a broader collective. That may range, for example, from the transaction between an individual's excerpted inkshedding text and another individual's reading it to the interaction between Inkshed and the rest of the scholarly community in Canada. Thus, I look at interactions and implications of those interactions as instances of being public, or publication.

I begin this discussion of publication by discussing the concept of what it means to be public, or the kinds of reactions that being public evokes. This is important because it helps to describe the experience of publication. The whole concept of publication is significant as a way of understanding the process described by Lave and Wenger (1991) of situated learning through legitimate peripheral participation (LPP). This chapter illustrates how movement to full participation requires movement to a more public sphere. The more one participates in a community, the more public one becomes. I illustrate this point, as I have in other chapters, with a vignette. In this scene, I describe my own publication experience, that is, the ways in which I was made public.

By describing my own publication as a human text, I reintroduce and make a connection between the issues of writing and membership.

I look at these from the perspective of an individual undergoing the process of becoming a member through textual interactions (both paper and human). I look at how interactions between individuals, and individuals and inkshedding texts, reflect membership. I follow this vignette with an exploration of inkshedding publication as a microcosm of publication in academia. This is important because it has implications for the way that membership develops in academic communities. In Inkshed, an academic community, tools or shared repertoire emerged as a result of interactions and engagement. In the final section of this chapter, I examine shared repertoire or tools for achieving joint enterprise. In other words, I look at the published inkshedding texts as representations or embodiments of a fuller, more central participation in the collective. I discuss the ways in which these published texts typify tools for membership within the collective.

Being Public

The first time that I, as a member of a disciplinary field, had a written text published for the rest of the field to read was an article in *Inkshed*, the community's newsletter (Horne, 2004). The day that the newsletter came out, I had several emails from Inkshedders telling me how much they had enjoyed my article. It was, not surprisingly, a great feeling to have members of the Inkshed community acknowledge my contribution. It made me feel like my piece was worthwhile, which, in turn, raised my personal feelings of worth and strengthened my feeling of connection with the community. As I will discuss later in this chapter, these feelings of success mirror some of the same kinds of feelings that took place in the inkshedding stage of publication. Just as I felt positive and encouraged by my first publication in academia, my ability to publish in inkshedding activities also made me feel like I had something valuable to contribute and it made me feel good about what I was doing. In describing the positive side of going public in the inkshedding process, Anthony Paré described one kind of encouraging reaction to publishing an Inkshed text. He said:

> It's always the same, right? I mean, "Hey that sounds pretty good." It turns out actually to have a pretty nice ring to it. Or somebody picks it up and says, "Somebody wrote this morning—," and reads your piece, and that's wow, that's fame in the Inkshed universe. (Personal interview, 12/5/2006)

As Anthony's comment illustrates, positive feelings accompany a sense of having been able to connect with the readership. Publishing at an Inkshed conference was in some ways a marker of the ways that individuals managed to engage with and participate successfully in the collective. I explore this concept in more detail in the last section of this chapter. I raise the point now, however, to illustrate the positive kinds of feelings that publication typically evokes. The individual response is likely to be positive and self-congratulatory and to serve as a builder of self-esteem. However, not all publishing evokes positive feelings. My first publishing experience was not limited to positive feelings about my accomplishment. It was also punctuated with feelings of exposure and lack of privacy.

The same day my article appeared, I received an email from an Inkshed listserv member whom I had never met. He was working in Utah and asked if he could quote part of my article in a chapter he was writing that dealt with spirituality and religion in composition processes. His request took me by surprise. Although not Mormon himself, he was living, working, and writing in a community that was largely Mormon. Two identities, Mormon and academic—that I typically worked hard to keep separate—were spinning together. Although my article, that described the spiritual nature of the experience I had at my first Inkshed talent show, said nothing wrong about Mormons, it also did not promote traditional Mormon values. It was not a paper I shared with my family or friends at church. And yet, through this connection, my academic self was being made public among Mormons, and there was nothing I could do about it. I had never considered the implications of the root word for publication—public. I was out there, and there was no turning back.

I had another public experience as a result of the same article a few months later when I attended a graduate course at McGill University. I was surprised by the way I had become public, known. The first evening of class we all went around the room and introduced ourselves. The course was multidisciplinary, with students from a broad variety of faculties, so when it was my turn I said, "I'm Miriam and I'm working on a PhD here in the Faculty of Education and I'm studying writing." The professor, whom I had never met, interrupted to ask if I was Miriam Horne. Taken aback that I was not anonymous, I said that I was, and she responded that she had enjoyed reading my article. I was staggered. Normally a private person, I was unprepared for the ways that my article had made me public and I found it made me uncomfortable.

Similarly, a few months after that, I attended a lecture in a series presented by the McGill Centre for the Study and Teaching of Writing. I was invited to join the organizer, speaker and another professor for lunch. As introductions were made, the professor said, "Miriam Horne, oh yes, I've heard of you." Like the other professor, she had heard of me because of my article in *Inkshed*.

These experiences taught me that publishing is not simply about having a contribution to the discipline recognized and feeling great that other members of a discipline think that you have something worthwhile to say. It is also, as I have described in my experiences above, a movement to a public place where personal boundaries and ideas about privacy are reexamined.

Once my first article was published, I was out there. I could not go back and unpublish the article and slip back into privacy and anonymity. Similarly, in inkshedding, once a text was published, there was no way of taking it back. Sometimes this meant feeling dissatisfied with what one had written and wishing to be able to clarify. In a discussion I had with one newcomer to Inkshed, she lamented the fact that the discussion had to take place on paper because she was unable to explain what she had been writing and felt that the excerpted section had been so decontextualized that her message was misconstrued (Field notes, 8/5/2004). Anthony Paré also described this discomfort by explaining:

> You may even go, "God, that is so stupid. What was I thinking?" And you may want to explain what you meant. But you can't. It's out there. And again, it's very similar to writing in the world, right? It's a broader world. You've got it out there now. You can't walk around behind the people reading, saying, "What I really meant was—." (Personal interview, 12/5/2006)

In addition to discomfort arising from misinterpretation or a sense of perfectionism that made individuals unhappy with what they had written, an even worse feeling came from not being published. Despite Russ Hunt's annual explanation of how to inkshed, in which he claimed it did not matter what you wrote, the academic community valued publication. Failure to perform in this way meant failure, and failure feels bad. As Nan Johnson pointed out:

> If they feel bad, that's one of the down sides [of inkshedding]. It really is. People feel bad when nothing they've written gets marked or gets published. People feel bad . . . . You have to think about the human level of it. You know, people do feel bad. (Focus group interview, 5/13/2005)

Thus, publication at an Inkshed conference was a complex stage, full of conflicting emotions. It was a highly charged experience regardless of the outcome. In the following vignette, I describe the ways in which publication of different kinds of texts took place—the text of Miriam and the text of a presentation I did at the 2006 Inkshed conference—and how this impacted my membership in the community.

Vignette

February 2006, I receive an email from the organizer of this year's Inkshed conference following up my proposal for a presentation with an invitation to speak for 30-40 minutes. The following week I receive another email—this one with a tentative conference schedule. I am taken aback to see my presentation scheduled first thing Friday morning of the conference with a time allotment of an hour and fifteen minutes. I check with the organizing committee on this to make sure it's not a misprint. I am assured it is correct—a 45-minute presentation with 30 minutes for inkshedding and discussion. I feel a pressure of responsibility weighing down on me. I have promised to speak about historical contexts for inkshedding.

When I arrive in Winnipeg a few months later, I am happy to be there. I am happy to reconnect with old acquaintances. As soon as I see Russ and Anne come into the dining room at suppertime, I jump up and greet them in an exchange of hugs. I make new acquaintances too—some new to Inkshed, others who have been around but I haven't had the chance to meet yet. I am comfortable and confident and enjoy the opening night book launch and socializing.

Friday morning my heart rate is a little faster than I would like as I feel some nervousness about how my presentation will be received. I am the first presenter. I spend breakfast recruiting people to participate. I have prepared my presentation as a dialogue with voices from the past and want audience members to read the different parts. I am hopeful that by giving the words of Inkshedders like Russ Hunt and Jim Reither to different voices in a different context, that I can evoke new perspectives on the history of Inkshed and inkshedding.

I think the presentation goes smoothly. Everyone gets their cues, and there are no major mishaps. After the inkshedding we have a discussion and I have the first feedback on how the presentation has been received. One woman, in preface to her question, tells me I have given "a quintessential Inkshed presentation." That is, I have given her a headache because of the self-reflection I've required of the audience.

Throughout the weekend, I continue to get bits of feedback here and there. Lines from the presentation weave into other conversations, become inside jokes, circulate. By lunchtime on Friday Janice Freeman is rallying a group of Inkshedders to prepare "Inkshed: The Opera" for the talent show—inspired by the tensions alluded to in my presentation. As a result, I find myself on stage Saturday night with several other brave (and somewhat intoxicated) Inkshedders clad in gold and velvet hastily acquired at the dollar store along with a plastic Viking helmet and singing the Inkshed version of "Ride of the Valkieries" ("Listen to Russ, Listen to Russ, Listen to Russ, Listen to Russ . . ."). Our opera ends with a dramatic death scene, the libretto for which comes directly from my presentation. We bow to roaring applause.

Sunday morning we prepare to wrap up the conference. Russ has been assigned to "pull it all together." When he begins to speak, he makes an allusion first to the wonderful job that Nan Johnson did the year before in her summary discussion of that conference. Russ explains that he is unable to do what Nan did so eloquently and didn't know quite how to go about doing this. So he decided "to take a page out of Miriam's book." He has typed up some of the published Inksheds from the weekend and incorporated them in an overview of the conference. He gives us each a part to read, just as I did in my presentation.

My ideas have fed back into the larger conversation. I have no doubt that I belong. I am an Inkshedder.

In the preceding vignette, I described the way that pieces of my presentation were published, or made public. In much the same way that pieces of inkshedding texts were excerpted and recirculated in the discussion, aspects of my presentation (both content and form) were picked up and reinserted into the ongoing dialogue of the conference. This happened through interactions like conversations over coffee and meals, but also through the talent show and Russ Hunt's choice of approach for his wrap-up presentation.

As I pointed out in an earlier chapter, newcomers who felt vulnerable felt anxious because they were in a peripheral position in the community and were trying to connect in meaningful ways with the collective. This vignette illustrates the ways that my public text resonated with the audience and was therefore successful. Those texts that were published (textual and human) gained successful public status because they connected in some meaningful way (as my presentation did) with the collective.

In addition to the ways that bits of my presentation continued to be public even after I finished, I also felt like bits of the text of Miriam were also being made public, circulated, and reinserted into the dialogue: Miriam, the researcher of inkshedding—opening speaker, 45-minute presentation; Miriam the performer—stand in front of people and present an academic presentation as easily as perform in a silly and light-hearted opera; Miriam the mother—"take these Viking helmets home to your kids." And on goes the list. And although at my first Inkshed Ann Beer highlighted the Miriam as researcher of Inkshed, over the years of my participation, these aspects I listed above all became published texts—the ones that got fed back into the ongoing dialogue. In the Burkean parlour, through participation, I became a full participant.

One of the important things about describing the publication experience in inkshedding, or in the Inkshed community in general, is the way in which it mirrored the kinds of publication experiences that take place in academia. In the following section, I look at this mirror and the reflections it offers on the importance of writing and community membership.

Academic Publication

The publication stage of the inkshedding process is, in many ways, a microcosm for the same kinds of publication experiences and processes that take place in the academy. This is important because it helps to describe the intensity of the final stage of inkshedding. In an interview, Anthony Paré explained his view of this parallel. He said:

I have always felt, from the very beginning, the great thing about Inkshed, in the little community settings, in the conference settings, is that it is an absolutely perfect microcosm of academic and scholarly work. There is a conversation ongoing; there is something to which other people are responding; you've heard more or less the same kinds of ideas; people write. A group of people sits and decides who's going to get to be published. It's so much like academic and scholarly life and it puts you in some of the same situations. You are going to side with people. You're going to go in—you have the whole kind of Burkean conversation. Someone says something; you side with them or you go against them; someone comes to your defense . . . . And I think that was one of the other things about it that was so appealing to me because here was this kind of microcosm of the academic world. And you could get written up; you could get published or *not* [emphasis his]. And it was life or death in the sense that it was so much like the publish or perish kind of situation that we all found ourselves in. (Personal interview, 12/5/2006)

The inkshedding process, as it was enacted at Inkshed conferences, reflected the publication process in academia. Just like an ongoing disciplinary conversation in academia, Inkshed facilitated a kind of conversation that people tried to join. Knowing how to join such a conversation and getting into it can be intimidating, and the interactions and introductions that newcomers have can influence participation therein. In academia, writing is assessed and reviewed by knowledgeable peers and members who fully participate in their disciplines. Success is seen when those peers agree to publish a document. Like gatekeepers, they decide who can enter. Peers who agree to publish a document are allowing the writer participation in the exclusive community of academia. Writers have been judged by their peers and accepted.

In inkshedding at conferences, comments that participants contributed to the conversation were also assessed and evaluated by peers in the discipline. Their contributions, or written comments, were first presented to peers during the second stage of inkshedding (circulation), and then they were assessed or reviewed by peers (usually) to establish whether or not something was valuable enough to be made public to the collective. A mark in the margin was a mark of acceptance and a determiner of who would be published.

The importance of publication in academia can be seen, for example, as graduate students finish their dissertations and attempt to join the academy as contributing members. One of the things that comes up as they try to establish themselves in their initial academic postings is how many presentations and how many publications they need to have before they can be considered established in the discipline (i.e., tenured). While no one in Inkshed counted or expected a minimum number of inkshedding publications from others, it is clear that, as in academia, success was measured by one's ability to publish. Lack of publications was a sign of failure. As one Inkshedder explained: "I think that's [sic] where the real pressure lies with inksheds as perhaps is also true with conference presentations generally is the need to elicit a response. Failure is measured by the lack of response" (Inkshedding text, 5/9/2004).

What this implies, then, is that in the same way publication is essential in gaining access to and maintaining membership in academic discourse communities, and is a marker of success, publication in Inkshed was an important part of membership. Although no record was kept of how many times a person published during a conference (indeed, the anonymity factor made this impossible), some individuals were well aware of their own publication record. The following comments illustrate this awareness: "In the ten years I've been coming I've been published less times than the number of fingers on one hand" (Field notes, 5/9/2004) and "Probably, for years, ten, twelve years, I never got anything published" (Focus group interview, 5/13/2005). The veteran Inkshedders who made these comments clearly counted their own number of publications. Similarly, it was not uncommon to skim the page of typed excerpts to see if one had "made it" before reading the other excerpts in detail (Field notes, 10/9/2004).

These comments, however, raise an interesting dilemma: I have been arguing that publication is a key element of membership but these remarks by long-time Inkshedders imply that membership even without publishing excerpted inkshedding texts was possible. In response to that I would argue that these individuals found other ways to publish within the community—and those not dissimilar to my own. Although their inkshedding texts were not published, their human texts were, at the very least, through their participation in the talent show that was held as a part of every conference. Like the inkshedding activity that exposed and made some people feel vulnerable, the talent show also put people on the spot and required risks. Like inkshedding, it required trust.

Both of the individuals I refer to above took major roles in the talent show and could always be relied on to perform and participate. Due to extenuating circumstances, I was unable to follow up with these individuals, but from my perspective, their participation in the community in ways beyond inkshedding facilitated their membership. Participation and being public through the talent show made them public—publications embodying the culture and values of the community. Membership in a collective does not come without being public in that collective.

Competition

In describing the inkshedding process, Russ Hunt explained: "The way this community has become a community has really been based on the notion that this is not about competing and savaging each other, but about responding to each other in dialogic ways" (Focus group interview, 5/13/2005). In many ways, the collegiality that Russ described was an important philosophy in the development and shaping of the community. Support and trust pulled community members together.

However, while this may be a shared ideology, the reality is getting published in inkshedding had a competitive side, as I pointed out in my discussion of the trashing that emerged from feeling vulnerable and the hidden power structures at play in the process of reading. Competition was evident in the following statements from Inkshedders:

> At subsequent Inkshed conferences, where we were invited to sign our inksheds, I sensed a competition to be recognized. (Inkshedding text, 5/9/2004)

> And I remember the very early Inksheds [i.e. conferences]. We used to make jokes—that were half serious—about, "Did I get published this time?" (Rick Coe, Focus group interview, 5/13/2005)

I'm competitive I suppose. And that part of it is also, that competitiveness, you know, can you get published? Do you want to put yourself in a situation where you might not get published and have to live with the disappointment? (Anthony Paré, Personal interview, 12/5/2006)

I like the idea [of the publication process], but it seems to smack of competition, quality control, etc. (Inkshed 2000 Live Archive, 2000)

These excerpts, from a variety of sources, point to the competitive nature of inkshedding. Although this perspective is contrary to the view that Russ Hunt embraced, the parallels to being successful in academia are clear—publish or perish, publish or remain on the periphery.

One manifestation of this competitive edge was that Inkshedders did not, in fact, simply write whatever came to mind (as initial instructions might suggest). Instead, they developed strategies that helped them to publish. As Anthony Paré explained: "If you could say something that nobody else was saying, your chances of being published were better" (Personal interview, 12/5/2006).

It was not until after several years' worth of conferences and using inkshedding in my classroom that I finally considered the possibility that there were certain strategies to inkshedding, but just like any genre, there were things that worked and things that did not. With this perspective in mind, at the next conference I attended I participated in inkshedding not with fear and anxiety, but with the specific intent to publish. Instead of beginning my responses with apologies or self indulgent excuses about my handwriting or what I had to say, I wrote short, succinct responses specific to the topic. My inkshedding was quick, legible, and focused on making connections with the theme of the conference in bite-sized bits rather than commiserating with the general readership on how hard inkshedding was, or going off on long, wandering ruminations.

I found that I wrote only when I had something to say; I did not write out of obligation or to be polite to the presenter, nor did I write to figure out what I wanted to say as is typical in a freewriting activity. My thoughts came across with clarity and precision. The result? From every text I wrote, something was excerpted and published. For example, after the opening presentation by Peter Vandenberg (who talked about graffiti as an alternative discourse), I wrote: "What strikes me is the way graffiti is being used as a tool of communication—in some cases being used in dialogic ways as it is put forth as an utterance—a meaningful, powerful statement expecting a response" (Inkshedding text, 5/3/2007).

With the knowledge I have now, it is not surprising to me, as it was in my early years of participation, that this was published. I used discipline- and community-specific language like "dialogic" and "utterance" and used the topic of graffiti from the presentation to comment on common values of the community—meaningful social interaction as shown in language like "communicate" and "meaningful."

At our closing dinner, one of the people recruited to type excerpts surprised me by saying: "You really knew what you were saying—you really got it. Lots of people didn't, but every time I read yours, I was like, yah" (Field notes, 5/5/2007).

As I described earlier, many newcomers were unaware of these kinds of strategies and therefore may have been less successful, that is, published minimally. As they learned how to write the things that effectively resonated with the collective, however, they successfully published and this led to feelings of membership.

Shared Repertoire and Membership

Researching the membership process in Inkshed as a participant observer (Lincoln & Guba, 1985) has given me a perspective on the process that I could not have gained as an outsider. It was only through participation that I came to understand that publication was a critical stage in inkshedding because it marked the success with which individuals negotiated membership. Either their fears and anxieties were realized and their fears about making meaningful connections were justified, or, their fears were allayed and they discovered that they had been able to share thoughts and ideas that resonated with the collective. Typically, this publication came in the form of excerpted inkshedding texts that were then circulated. These particular texts are the focus of this section. However, as I pointed out with the veteran Inkshedders who did not publish inkshed texts, but who took major parts in the talent show, I am also mindful of other kinds of publication—the human text through a conference presentation, speaking out in discussions, performing in talent night, or otherwise having a public interaction. In their own way, each of these instances reflected Inkshed values and the ways that Inkshedders engaged. In this section, however, I focus on inkshedding texts as tangible, conscientious, and purposeful tools for engagement.

Published inkshedding texts are a tangible realization of successful interactions or the ways that individuals engaged with the collective through the writing process. Engagement with the collective through inkshedding and the realization of that engagement through publication helped individuals identify with and feel part of the collective.

Consider the following comments written by Inkshedders in response to a presentation I gave about joining the Inkshed collective. I shared some of my experiences and asked for their responses as a way of confirming the things I was seeing (Patton, 2002). Confirming my own experiences, some Inkshedders connected success in inkshedding with membership. One person wrote: "I appreciated it when people did respond to what I wrote—that gave me confidence to write in this setting. I am very happy and eager to write in my professional settings" (Inkshedding text, 5/9/2004). Similarly, another wrote: "What happened was that my words were read and responded to, sometimes with agreement, sometimes with questions. And, in retrospect, I think it was the writing plus the responses that made me feel a member of the community" (Inkshedding text, 5/9/2004).

Both of these examples reflect the ways in which individuals made connections between engagement with the collective through the writing process and membership. Without specifically using the term "membership," the first comment referred to responses to the writing from the collective. The existence of responses illustrates the way that the writer was able to make meaningful connections with others. The writer linked this engagement with confidence in disciplinary discussions and thus recognized their own disciplinary identity or membership. The second example also reflects the importance of responses to writing—again, an illustration of the way the writer was able to engage. The writer went on to make a clear link between this engagement and membership in the Inkshed collective. Thus, as a representation of the ways that people have responded to texts, the published inksheds contribute to understanding how the inkshedding process facilitated membership. They served as a public acknowledgement of engagement with the author.

It is worth noting that this idea of publication seems to resonate with theories of writing as a social act in which writing takes place in particular social contexts. As I discussed in Chapter 2, over time, as situations recur, responses take on typified forms according to the values of the community. Publication in Inkshed illustrates this idea because published texts were responses that resonated with cultural values of the community and met its expectations. While no published text was identical to another, texts that resonated most with the community appeared as publications.

In addition, the centrality of these published texts to membership in the collective supports notions that Wenger (1998) used when describing characteristics of a community of practice. The texts are one example of shared repertoire—a term that Wenger (1998) used to describe the materials that emerge from and facilitate legitimate participation. Other examples of shared repertoire specific to Inkshed included the single-session conference format, the talent show, and the use of the listserv.

According to Wenger, materials like these typed-up texts that emerge from participation should be used to further the goal of the collective. In this case, the goal of the collective was to learn through mutual engagement, and the publishing aspect of the activity was specifically designed so that the text could be reinserted into the ongoing dialogue in order to stimulate more interactions. Thus, the text was only effective as a collective tool if it was reinserted into the ongoing discourse. The reinsertion of texts took place in a variety of ways that, when done correctly, facilitated the realization of continued dialogic interactions.

Timeliness

Depending on conference organizers, excerpted texts were usually distributed at break or meal times. Several times I arrived at breakfast to find a freshly printed page of inkshedding excerpts at my place, or to have one handed to me as I was eating. It was not enough, however, in establishing practices that form a CoP, to simply redistribute the texts, or hand out the tools for mutual engagement. The tools had to be used. The texts had to find their way back into the ongoing conversation. Meal and break times facilitated discussion of texts because people had free time and were together to talk. Nan Johnson described the way that this can happen when she said:

> This is one of the great things about it, right? People sat at breakfast and read those this morning, and more conversation happened. And I said, at my table, "you know, I always forget how good this part is." Right? Because everybody reads and then everybody's talking about it all over again. That's very cool. That's very cool when that happens. (Focus group interview, 5/13/2005)

Texts also got pulled in through presentations and other discussions. In an earlier example in this chapter, I quoted Anthony Paré and he alluded to how the texts were reinvested. He said: "Somebody picks it up and says, "somebody wrote this morning—" (Personal interview, 12/5/2006). Similarly, in a personal conversation (Field notes, 5/8/2004), Kenna Manos explained to me that it was common to hear allusions to published inkshedding texts throughout the conference in presentations and discussions. In other words, texts were often directly quoted or referred to as ways of supporting, challenging, or otherwise enhancing ongoing dialogue.

As these examples describe, the texts were inserted in the conversation in virtually the same time and space in which they were written—removed from their creation by only an hour or two. Immediate and timely insertion of these texts was critical if they were going to facilitate engagement and participation. At one conference, the published texts did not arrive until the following day, and when they did, there were only single copies. People had to mill around one large table to read them. It was so crowded that many did not read them at all. Others complained that they were unable to write on their own copies. Describing the problem, Kenna Manos observed:

> the first set of Inksheds was not ready (I'm not entirely sure that I'm right here) until Sunday morning (or was it Saturday night?) and then there was only a single set of the things. There were multiple copies of the later ones, but many people had already left by that point. Unlike other years, the Inksheds did not feed into the rest of the conference. In fact, I didn't hear anyone refer to a previous Inkshed in subsequent sessions. (Personal communication, 5/15/2004)

Similarly, Russ Hunt (2004) explained the importance of timeliness when he wrote:

> They [published inkshedding texts] need to be circulated immediately, and used. The older an inkshed is, the staler. It has a short shelf life. Serve it fresh or not at all. A good way to dramatize that inksheds are

not quick ways to generate permanent texts, but are rather ways to render text conversational, is to throw them away when they've served their function—that is, when they've been read and had an effect on the social situation in which they arose.

In other words, if texts were not immediately used as tools for generating discussion and dialogic interactions, then they ceased to be useful tools.

Thus, immediacy of time and place helped to reinsert inkshedding texts into the ongoing dialogue. That being said, however, there were some exceptions. For example, in preparing the presentation that I described in the earlier vignette, I drew heavily on inkshedding excerpts done in response to a presentation I made two years earlier. The texts were definitely taken out of their time, but they were written about inkshedding and I was using them to continue to talk about inkshedding and so they fed back into the presentation in meaningful ways. I have also used these excerpts liberally throughout this document, in conference presentations at the Canadian Association for the Study of Discourse and Writing (CASDW) and the Conference on College Composition and Communication (CCCC), and even in job talks in an effort to insert inkshedding into a larger academic discussion about writing and membership.

Intertextuality

So far, my description of published texts being reinserted has been limited to the tangible paper and ink publications. However, as my vignette suggests, and as I have argued elsewhere in this book, in the Inkshed community the human text followed processes parallel to those of an inkshedding text in its circulation and publication. In a similar way human interactions were also reinserted—some, as my vignette suggested, in the conference and the way that people contributed as members to the collective. However, also in the same way that I have used inkshed texts to expand conversations outside the ones in which they were created, published human texts crossed boundaries into other conversations as well, creating an intertextuality between potentially different genres.

In the previous chapter I talked about how people as texts were marked. These highlighted sections of individuals reflected the ways people interacted and were a public statement of that interaction. The markings became part of individuals' identities and they carried the markings with them across boundaries. "Inkshed: The Opera" provides a simple example of this. Although I contributed to the opera at the talent night, I participated with others who marked me. The experience stood out and I came home talking about it. Extra Viking helmets were rounded up so that my kids could each have a helmet and "Inkshed: The Opera" crossed the boundary of Inkshed the conference and has been inserted into my family dialogue and lore of stories we tell. Even now, years later, the helmets continue to get much use and the stories continue to be retold. Because of my shared identity as an Inkshedder and mother and the links that join the two worlds, it was natural to insert the light side of "Inkshed: The Opera" into family discussions, and even into family practices such as wearing helmets around the house. Two sets of values, two sets of practices, and two sets of language intertwined.

This crossing of boundaries, like the example I used in the vignette in which I described a blurring of borders between my intellectual and spiritual lives, or my discussion earlier in this chapter of being public, suggests that learning influences people not just in the spaces in which they expect to learn, but also in a variety of aspects of their lives. This has implications for LPP (Lave & Wenger, 1991) in which learning seems to be deliberate and purposeful.

One of the things that set CASLL apart from CASDW or other similar kinds of academic associations was the intimate way in which learning took place. As Anthony Paré suggested: "Inkshed/CASLL, probably more than any other such communities, affects people intimately—that is, at a personal level usually not much considered in intellectual life" (Personal communication, 5/17/2007).

Although the example of "Inkshed: The Opera" is a simple one, it serves to illustrate an important idea about humans as texts. People, unlike the written texts (which remained, for the most part, contextualized in the conference), continued to circulate and take part in a variety of conversations. The marks that they acquired in an Inkshed conference carried with them to other conversations and influenced understandings, interpretations, and discussions in other settings and vice versa. Thus, a variety of memberships shaped and highlighted aspects of individual identities.

Just as each stage of inkshedding was important to membership, it also had a down side—a side that did not engage or achieve its goals. Despite the successful ways that many inkshedding texts were reinserted into ongoing dialogues and full participation was achieved, some texts went no further than the back of the file folder in the bottom of the Inkshed bag. This lack of engagement sometimes led to questioning of tradition and the way that things were made public in Inkshed. However, my experiences suggest that although questions arose, they did not facilitate change of tradition.

Questioning

In the previous chapter I mentioned a woman who was frustrated by the fact that nothing she wrote ever got published. In her frustration, she wrote an inkshedding text asserting that only certain kinds of things were publishable and that writing "outside the box" of Inkshed made it impossible to publish (Field notes, 5/9/2004). According to her recollections of her first Inkshed conference, it was only after she wrote her text that pushed at or questioned Inkshed tradition that people responded to her writing. When the woman shared this anecdote in a larger group discussion, others immediately jumped in and tried to dispel this uncomfortable perspective by sharing anecdotes of their own lack of publication. Their anecdotes were not shared as a way of agreeing with her, but almost, it seemed, as if her concerns were unjustified. Often this was done in an almost humorous, self-deprecating way as if to suggest (without blatantly contradicting her) that she had over-reacted (Field notes, 5/9/2004). That is, by responding with anecdotes of "I've been published less than five times in ten years!" (Field notes, 5/9/2004), those who defended inkshedding suggested that the woman's concern with publication was overly sensitive and unwarranted.

What this example illustrates is that despite a sometimes idyllic self-promotion of the community, some participants found aspects of the activity and collective disturbing and questionable, but voicing of these feelings did not guarantee change. Another example describes a cautious approach to questioning tradition. Describing frustration with reading excerpted texts, one person wrote: "I don't know about the inkshed we just got—everything seemed difficultly decontextualized—maybe we need to do more sharing in context in small groups" (Inkshed 2000 Live Archive, 2000). In this statement lies the suggestion that the inkshedding activity as it took place in this instance was not working effectively. Excerpted inksheds could not be reinserted into discussion because they were too decontextualized to be meaningful. The suggestion was that dialogue needed to happen through more discussion. However, the suggestion was couched in tentative, non-aggressive language—carefully inoffensive. That this sentiment resonated with others in the group was clear from the fact that this piece was excerpted and circulated. The tension between talking and writing continued to be an issue to varying degrees. Each conference I attended had some discussion of how much inkshedding to do or how much discussion to have in general, yet no resolution was ever reached.

Since published inkshedding texts did not move out of time and place, they were sometimes perceived as self-congratulatory, self-indulgent, self-promoting, and did not, in a spirit of critical inquiry, enact change. Some people found this frustrating and chose not to participate in this community.

Published texts, however, must be understood not just as tools for facilitating conversation but as symbols of something more. Barton (2000) described one aspect of a literacy event (a way of talking about interactions that take place around a text) as an artifact. The term "artifact" is especially appropriate here because it implies a kind of stasis in time and does not change—much like the inkshedding texts that lose their meaning when decontextualized. However, like artifacts dug up by archaeologists as symbols, representations, and embodiments of cultures, values, and practices, the published inkshedding excerpts contributed to the community by what they represented. The text was an embodiment of the interactions that a text underwent. It was a realization of the ways that an individual successfully used language to engage with the collective. The published inkshedding text was a symbol of that engagement and therefore was a symbol of belonging.

Like the questions raised about the usefulness or purpose of inkshedding texts, the way Inkshed as a Canadian academic association publishes itself within Canada has been questioned. However, Inkshed as an organization is also an important symbol. Some people believe that Inkshed has not done enough for publication in Canada; by publication I am referring to the ways that CASLL participates in and contributes to the broader disciplinary conversation of writing studies in Canada. Although the community published the occasional book that made a contribution to writing studies, some people felt that the community needed to do more and should have taken a more active role in writing studies. For example, Tania Smith (2000), as part of the conclusion to her ethnographic study of Inkshed, raised the following questions about Inkshed's public presence:

> My complaint is that it just doesn't seem to do things *as* a group in arenas *outside* the group. It's presently a very good club, a camp, an exciting and stimulating yearly experience, a shed devoted to the mutual encouragement of people working in discourse and education. It does this well for many members that return again and again. But can you join me for a moment in wishing that Inkshed could seem to do more, that it could be more visible to outsiders, that Inkshed would earn a reputation as an association that does something important and good in Canada?

Tania felt that Inkshed was not being public enough in Canada and that as an association it needed to do more. This, too, was an issue that occasionally got discussed, but very little changed. At the 2006 conference a proposal was brought to the AGM to look into the possibility of setting up a network with other similar organizations in order to facilitate things like funding. Although the members at the AGM eventually agreed that this could be looked into without committing to any action, even this agreement to look into a potential change was met with resistance. One veteran Inkshedder voiced his stance that Inkshed should remain small and focused on pedagogy. He was clearly concerned that this proposal might lead to a change in the nature of Inkshed (Field notes, 5/14/2006).

Despite the veteran Inkshedder's assertion that Inkshed needed to stay as it was in order to meet the needs of its members, questions about the viability of the community were also raised. In response to a presentation I gave, one person wrote:

> I was wondering about the Inkshed community and its viability—if the practice of inkshedding serves the purpose of developing and sustaining this community of Inkshedders, is it perhaps on the wane? If Inkshedders themselves do not use it in their own classrooms, and if the number of Inkshed members is dwindling, is it perhaps time for Inkshedding to give way to other types of community-building practices? (Inkshed 23, 2006)

When I included this excerpt on the listserv with a question about the community's future, it was met with a resounding discussion (from long-time and well-established Inkshedders) affirming the community's role and viability. For example, Roberta Lee wrote:

> The validity of the community does not depend on the various ways that inkshedding is or is not used . . . . In addition, I have appreciated the quality of the dialogue and the way in which those who participate are respected as equals, whatever their "credentials."

This kind of support and encouragement serves as a powerful antidote to the competitive and hierarchical nature of academia. Could it be that this unique Canadian community is needed more today than ever before? (CASLL Listserv, 12/14/2006)

This response was typical of the kinds of postings to the listserv that both validated and promoted the Inkshed community. Thus, like inkshedding texts that Russ Hunt (2004) suggested could be thrown away immediately after a discussion, Inkshed, as a public domain, did not appear to carry forward. Criticisms and questions were met with resounding testimonials of why the status quo must be maintained. One original Inkshedder admitted: "I have been going for such a long time—and loving the way it's traditionally been done—that there's always a danger that my ideas may be resistant to change" (Personal correspondence, 6/2/2004). While those who lauded Inkshed did so with reason, to others, this kind of stasis constituted weakness. The fact that the community had recently put its annual conference on hold, seeking to redefine itself, suggests that perhaps the changes were more necessary than some members were willing to admit.

However, like the published texts that, as artifacts, represent a history of mutual engagement, negotiation, and creation of meaning, the Inkshed community embodies a history, a way of thinking, and a way of understanding the world. In her article on genres, Schryer (1994) described them as, "stabilized-for-now or stabilized enough sites of social and ideological action" (p. 108). This description rings true of Inkshed. For twenty-five years, Inkshed was a stabilized community whose practices and actions reflected social and ideological values. These values remain stable and carry forward even without the benefit of an annual conference—the listserv, newsletter and other networking opportunities continue to reinforce Inkshed values. While not everyone chooses or feels like they can be members of the collective, those who do, do so passionately.

Summary

Publication, or movement to a place in which interactions are publicly acknowledged, is a realization of community membership. This publication happens at a variety of levels; in the case of Inkshed, it happened from publication of an inkshedding text that had been circulated among peers to the publication of an individual who had been acknowledged and accepted by her peers. In Inkshed, and dare I add the broader scope of academe, publication serves as a marker for both the individual and the collective that the individual has made a valuable contribution to the community, understands the community values, and therefore, for at least that moment, is a member of the community.

Publication is an embodiment of belonging and a tool for creating and maintaining this community of practice. In addition, publication is a stage in which a writer is given full responsibility for participation and that participation is legitimized by the collective. That is, from the perspective of LPP, the individual who publishes has successfully learned to participate and has moved from a position of peripheral participation to full participation. The community acknowledges this successful movement by making the text public.

Through my examination of the stages culminating in this final stage of publishing, a clearer image begins to emerge of the ways that writing processes facilitate community membership. I sought to explore the ways in which collective writing processes (i.e., socially mediated writing practices of communities) facilitate newcomer membership. This chapter reflects the outcome of the inkshedding process, the outcome of the learning process, and the ways that I, as a newcomer, successfully learned to participate in the Inkshed community of practice. I believe that many of these experiences resonate with experiences outside of the Inkshed community and represent common experiences of those working outside of Inkshed in the greater scope of academia.

In the final chapter, I reflect on the implications of my work and the lessons that I have learned along the way.

6

Membership: Lessons Learned

F*all 2009, Champlain College, Burlington, Vermont—I find myself thinking about a conversation I had a few days ago with a colleague about a mutual first year student. "She's scared to death of writing," he told me. "She's afraid that if someone else in the class reads her writing, they'll laugh at her and make fun of her." His description of what the student said and her angst rings home to me. I can tell by the tone in his voice that he thinks it's ludicrous to be so insecure, but I know. I know how debilitating her fear is. I know how marginal she feels. I know how hard it is to write into a new community. But I also know that if I can get her to take a risk, she'll probably be okay.*

It wasn't so long ago that I was that student—so fearful, so insecure, so afraid of being discovered as an impostor. A friend laughed when I told him that and spent an hour trying to tell me why my feelings were irrational. But now, here I sit in my office that overlooks the beautiful

Lake Champlain. My diploma hangs on my wall, my desk is littered with various proposals, presentations and articles I'm working on, and stacks of student assignments awaiting my attention continue to grow in my "to do" box. My calendar is overflowing with student conferences, committee meetings, and appointments. All the written signs are here indicating that I have successfully negotiated my way into academia, and, more specifically, the discipline of writing studies.

My students see only the outcome. They are unaware of the process of learning that got me here. I represent a world that is unfamiliar and foreign. But we are not so far removed from each other. I have not yet shaken my insecurities about writing in academia, but I have learned to take risks and grow from them. Abby [pseudonym], my student, hasn't learned the value of risks yet. She hasn't learned that only by taking chances will she be successful here.

As I prepare to head off to my first year Rhetoric course I am mindful of the insecurities Abby has voiced that represent so many of her classmates. They haven't learned yet to join this academic community. They're still nervous and shy and their writing shows that they don't understand why they're writing. They don't realize that this is the introduction to their conversation now. It's my job to teach them how to participate, to give them a safe place to take risks, and to get them participating in meaningful ways so that their texts will be "published" and they too can be successful in their disciplines.

The initial inkshedding experience I described at the beginning of this book served to set into motion a series of events and circumstances that allowed me to participate in academia in meaningful and legitimate ways. The way I learned to participate in the Inkshed community gave me a position in a larger academic conversation in which I now participate in my role as assistant professor at Champlain College.

And I am mindful that many of my incoming first year students share the same needs and angst that I had so many years ago. The difference is, now I understand. I understand that joining a community is risky and uncomfortable. I understand that it is not just my written text that is circulated as part of an academic conversation (whether through inkshedding texts, or articles and proposals submitted to journals and conferences) but it is also me that is circulating. I am putting myself out there to be read and commented on. It takes courage; it takes trust; it takes conviction. But here I am—a successful and participating member of academe. I have not, however, forgotten my angst. Therefore, as I work with my first year students, I am sensitive to where they are and to the first steps they are taking to join the academic community.

The attitude with which I approach my students and my writing illustrates the support that this study gives to notions of writing as a social practice. The people and circumstances in which writing occurs also drive its creation. This attitude also points, however, to the idea that practice is essential to belonging and reinforces Wenger's (1998) theory of communities of practice (CoPs) However, I add depth to the theory by addressing human realities that can both help and hinder membership in communities. Finally, writing shapes identity. As texts circulate, they are read and marked upon, and as human texts are written on, they grow and take on different identities.

Writing is a Social Practice

One of the concepts that drove this study was to understand an underlying motivation for inkshedding—that is, to explore the idea that writing is a social act. Scholars in writing studies have explained that writing takes place within socially situated contexts, has meaning within those contexts, and is shaped within those contexts (Bazerman, 1994; Dias, Freedman, Medway & Paré, 1999; Miller, 1984). In turn, different writing forms and practices shape the communities that develop and use them (Devitt, 2004; Paré & Smart, 1994). This research reinforces notions of writing as a social act as shown in the work of Dias et al. (1999) who argued that:

> Writing is seldom the product of isolated individuals but rather and seldom obviously, the outcome of continuing collaboration, of interactions that involve other people and other texts. Writing practices are closely linked to their sociocultural contexts and writing strategies vary with individual and situation. (p. 10)

Additionally, this research resonates with claims of genre scholars who ". . . connect a recognition of regularities in discourse types with a broader social and cultural understanding of language in use" (Freedman & Medway, 1994, p. 1). In other words, this work supports the work of those like Miller (1984), Freadman (1994), Schryer (1994), Paré (2002), Artemeva (2006), and others who have worked so hard to locate writing within social structures and understand texts as being socially generated. My research supports this work not just by reaffirming it—that is, by discussing the social need for and creation of inkshedding texts which in turn feed back into the community—but by adding to it through exploring the human element that accompanies these texts. If we are to truly understand writing as a social act, then we must also understand the very real demands and anxieties that this action may generate. Understanding the struggles and triumphs of learning to write in a community can do much to further understandings of membership and identity. As social action, writing practices engaged in by the Inkshed community were at times angst-filled and challenging. However, they also reflected community values and embodied community specific language, the learning of which facilitated community. The activities also helped to formalize or concretize a sometimes fuzzy or vague notion of audience.

Social Values and Language

Those who understand writing as a social act understand that while each social circumstance is unique, commonalities recur. In the case of Inkshed, for example, each conference was unique but had recurring commonalities like single sessions, inkshedding, and a talent night. In part, these recurring situations were based on values that determined the situations and appropriate responses in those situations. This study of inkshedding and Inkshed illustrates the ways that social values were embedded within the writing practices in which the community engaged.

Inkshedding worked within the Inkshed community because the community valued dialogic interaction and continued learning, but they also valued trust, friendship, and safety. Inkshedding worked for this community because it embodied these same values. In the early years, when inkshedding was used as a tool for trashing, it failed to function as a dialogic interaction because the trust, friendship, and safety were also missing. As inkshedding developed over the years, however, the values of trust and safety became more entrenched so that it became a dialogic interaction.

Values were reflected both in the writing practices and implicitly in the language being used. Through nontraditional presentations, inkshedding, and discussion the values of the community were manifest and reinforced. Each of these interactions required language and it is through language that values become entrenched in a community. Part of the embodiment of values is in language. Social constructionists talk about the way that language is used within communities to describe the knowledge they create. Bruffee (1986) explained that "[a] writer's language originates with the community to which he or she belongs. We use language primarily to join communities we do not yet belong to and to cement our membership in communities we already belong to" (p. 784).

According to this logic, as newcomers to Inkshed learned the language, they solidified their membership in the community, but this language and membership was closely tied up with the community values. Learning to use the language appropriately reflects the ways in which members understand values. Throughout this book I have made reference to literacy events, literacy practices, and social structures associated with literacy as a way of pointing to the centrality of language in a community of practice. I have talked about the ways practices cross borders to help make sense of inkshedding, the centrality of inkshedding as an event leading to dialogic interaction, and the ways that power structures influenced participation in inkshedding. Barton and Hamilton (2005), Tusting (2005), and Creese (2005) all argued that lack of attention to literacy and language constituted a weakness in Wenger's (1998) explication of CoPs. The absence of language in his theory, they argued, does not allow for a free understanding of social processes. Language and its use were central in my observations and participation in Inkshed. Language was both a fundamental value and tool for the Inkshed community. Thus, I reinforce the position of Barton and Hamilton, Tusting, and Creese, and underscore the role of language as a tool for participation and therefore membership in the community.

When I first began attending Inkshed conferences, I had to concentrate and focus to be able to understand what the presenters were saying and I struggled to make meaning from their words. Although I knew most of the words they were using, I was unable to understand how they were using them. As I have learned the language of writing studies, however, my understanding and ability to participate in Inkshed have been facilitated. For example, terms like "genre" and "rhetoric" are not uncommon words in the English language and they appear fairly regularly. In spite of this commonness, the way that these words are used within writing studies carries a different shade of meaning from other contexts such as, for example, a book reviewer for a newspaper describing the genre of the book being critiqued, or a news reporter talking about a politician's rhetoric. In writing studies, these words come laden with dynamic meanings that are constantly being redefined, reunderstood, and reconceptualized as writing studies moves forward. Within Inkshed, this was equally so. The term "genre" and the way Inkshedders used it was heavily influenced by the works of Canadian genre scholars (e.g., Artemeva & Freedman, 2006; Freedman & Medway, 1994; Paré, 2002; Paré & Smart, 1994; Schryer, 1994) where it was coupled with notions of dialogism.

Based on my experiences, I found that understanding this language and being able to use the language appropriately facilitated membership. I can still clearly remember my feeling of amazement at the last conference I attended when I realized that I understood all the presentations and discussions. I did not have to squint my eyes and stare at their mouths and visual aids in a desperate effort to focus on and understand the vocabulary the presenters used. As terms like "genre," "discourse," and "rhetorical analysis" washed over me, I found that I now understood. I did not have to concentrate so hard on understanding the way the words were being used. I could concentrate on making connections between what each presenter said, the other presentations, the theme of the conference, and my own work. As a result, when it came time to participate in inkshedding, I was a stronger participant. I was able to focus my ideas into bite-size pieces using the language of the community. In addition, I was able to carry on oral conversations and further ideas in that way as well.

This was a far different position than I found myself in at my first conference where I felt vulnerable and insecure. I began in the peripheral position that Lave and Wenger (1991) described—able to participate in a limited way. As my language and understanding of the culture grew, so did my participation. Learning the language of the community and the appropriate ways in which to use it—understanding the exigence of the situation—helped me participate and therefore become a member of the community. Thus, as we seek to understand the ways in which communities function and develop, we must be sensitive to the language being used as a way to reinforce and foster deeper understanding of the community.

The social process of language requires human participation. It is not enough to understand writing as located within community, but we must understand that communities are made up of individuals who shape and are shaped by their individual strengths and insecurities. Sometimes these individual characteristics will gravitate toward each other, as I believe happened in the case of Inkshed; compassionate, caring, and passionate individuals found resonance in their feelings of isolation in the broader academic context. To facilitate this very human connection, language is used to hold meaning for values, priorities, and relationships. Learning the language of a community can help individuals to understand the forces that drive it.

Practice Essential to Belonging

Understanding a human element to writing and the dynamic nature of language facilitates understanding community membership. If writing is a social act, then there are social structures in place to shape that writing. By learning to write in ways appropriate for a particular social group, individuals may gain membership into that group. This seems especially relevant to academia where writing is a key to success.

In order for writing to be an effective tool for community membership, writers must be willing to engage in the practices. It is not enough merely to observe. There must be, as Lave and Wenger (1991) pointed out, opportunities for legitimate participation—at first peripheral, but meaningful nevertheless.

Publication, or full membership in, or an acknowledgement from peers of an ability to take part in the collective discussion, comes about only from participation. As a graduate student, I attended a variety of academic conferences from CCCC to TESOL to CASDW and even a few others. Although I presented at each of these conferences, I never felt connected or a member (despite paying dues) in the same way that I did at Inkshed. This is because Inkshed demanded participation and by participating in a variety of ways, I came to understand the values inherent in the language. Furthermore, I came to understand the other humans and their angsts and triumphs and how that shaped the community. By isolating participants from potential distractions and holding the conference in an isolated location, by running a single-session conference, by housing participants all together, and by ensuring lots of time to socialize as well as work together, and, of course, by writing together, Inkshed highlighted the need for participation in order to be published—participation in order to become a member.

When Wenger (1998) wrote that "collective learning results in practices that reflect both the pursuit of our enterprises and the attendant social relations" (p. 45) and that "these practices are thus the property of a kind of community created over time by the sustained pursuit of a shared enterprise" (p. 45), he explained how communities are formed through practices. My work that draws on the Inkshed community illustrates and reinforces this in a very vivid way. Inkshed community members engaged with each other to learn and that engagement led to inkshedding practices that reinforced learning.

Wenger's (1998) theory of CoPs points to the importance of practice in bringing people together in a community working toward a common goal. My research supports this notion. The practices of Inkshed are essential to its identity as a community and are essential in gaining membership. While it is possible to be an Inkshedder without practicing inkshedding, it is not possible to be an Inkshedder without embracing and practicing the philosophies behind inkshedding—that is, writing as socially constructive, as knowledge generating, as dialogic.

What I have come to understand about that first awkward attempt at writing in Anthony Paré's writing across the curriculum course, which I described in Chapter 1, was that, like any newcomer to a discipline or academia in general, when I began, I felt like I was in a peripheral position. I had been accepted to graduate school, but seriously questioned my abilities to perform adequately and succeed. When he introduced inkshedding to our class, Anthony asked us to do more than sit passively and go unnoticed in whatever place we were in. He asked us to participate. Over the two years that I was involved in inkshedding in a variety of courses at McGill, I was forced to participate in my classes, interact with my classmates, and otherwise take a place in my classroom community. This participation, although often uncomfortable, helped me to understand my classmates better—I came to know them more personally, to know their interests, to follow their studies, and to make connections when I might otherwise never have spoken with them. I gained confidence in my identity as a graduate student learning the discourse of academia as I participated in my classroom microcommunities. I tried ideas, had feedback from peers, and was never laughed at. It gave me a way of fitting in.

I recognize that this does not work for everyone. Perhaps what worked for me was that I lacked the drive to engage in other ways and needed the strong invitation that Inkshed presented and the dedicated requirements of participation. Other people rejected that invitation, but for me it worked. When I went to the Inkshed community, I was invited to participate in the community not just in inkshedding, but also in all the other dialogic kinds of activities available at the conference. I felt as though inkshedding and all the other activities were invitations to participate and engage. I was fortunate enough to have a strong and insistent invitation facilitated by my connection to original Inkshedder Anthony Paré, and by my research agenda. At times, newcomers to Inkshed felt like they were extended a polite invitation and then ignored. Although I respect this perspective and understand how the intensive nature of the conference might have led to this, it is not a perspective to which my experience led. I had an invitation to participate and did so. The result of my participation was identifying with other participants. I was given opportunity to and did connect in meaningful ways with other Inkshedders to the extent that I could identify with them and call myself an Inkshedder. The initial question of what makes inkshedding work I understand now as not a question about inkshedding per se, but as a way of understanding how participation in a collective leads to membership. Membership, both in graduate school classes and at Inkshed, gave me communities, and therefore, places to belong.

Writing Shapes Identity

I see identity as a process of taking on membership. The writing processes I have described in this book illustrate the ways that writing facilitated membership in Inkshed. As I learned to inkshed, I learned the language, values and practices of the community, and, more importantly, made them my own. I embraced them with the same belief and passion with which some embrace a religion. By inkshedding, I came to believe in its effectiveness as a tool for community and a tool for knowledge. As I have described throughout this book, writing brought me into the community, gave me a voice, and has now given me a scholarly identity.

That being said, however, I would suggest that my own concept and definition of identity is insufficient. The implication of understanding identity simply as a process of membership is that any individual can join multiple communities and have separate and multiple identities. This notion is clearly problematic. Various identities cannot be isolated from each other so the process of membership is often also a negotiation with other identities or memberships. This is best illustrated perhaps through the experience I described at my first talent night. I found myself identifying with the Inkshed community but was conflicted because the spiritual aspect that resonated with me had only been associated with my religious identity. In other words, identities cross borders.

Border Crossings

Betsy Sargent told me on more than one occasion that inkshedding was a spiritual experience for her. She linked the idea of practice with faith and a higher good. She wrote: "I think that, like meditation or daily exercise, inkshedding is discipline that one does even when one doesn't particularly feel like it, in the faith that the cumulative impact will do one nothing but good" (Personal communication, 12/14/2006). While for Betsy the idea of everyone sitting and writing together was deep and profound, I do not think that it was the activity itself that crossed the boundaries of academia into my private life; it was the outcome of the activity and the philosophy that drives it—that persistent quest to engage in meaningful dialogue.

Without going into doctrine or history, I think it is important to explain what I mean when I talk about spirituality. Mormons teach that any time you feel good, happy, content, or otherwise positive, this is a manifestation of the Holy Ghost. The manifestation of the Holy Ghost is like the presence of God, and therefore this constitutes a type of spiritual experience. Since my initial talent night when I felt a strong resonant connection with the spirit of the moment, I have had to reexamine my understanding of spirituality, the experiences I describe as spiritual, and what has made them so. My reexamination led to questions about God, primarily, "What does God care about inkshedding?" or "Why would God's presence be manifest at an Inkshed conference?" This has led to other questions about God and the role of God in my life and has also led me to reexamine other significant spiritual moments in my life. Without doing a completely exhaustive life review, some commonalities emerge fairly quickly. The majority of these experiences share two common things: a strong sense of womanhood—that is, there is usually a majority of women, and (as contradictory as it may seem) a patriarchal figure.

These commonalities are consistent with my Inkshed experiences. While I had not focused on it before, in a recent conversation, Roger Graves pointed out that in the course of its development, Inkshed had undergone a feminization. It should be noted that I use this term cautiously. I am aware that the term is imbued with meaning through gender studies, philosophy, history and other schools of thought that try to make meaning of the world. For my purposes, I use it not only because the majority of participants at the conference were women, but also because I would argue that the spirit of traditional male-dominated agonism and competition that led to some of the trashing in early years has given way to a spirit of support, sometimes even nurturing, caring and other characteristics typically assigned to females.

Whereas a traditional academic conference is set up in an agonistic kind of way, with the presenter on the spot and under fire to hold ideas up to careful scrutiny, presenters at an Inkshed conference found themselves part of a larger intellectual endeavour. That is, they worked not individually, but as part of a whole to make meaningful connections. In the attempt to make people feel welcome and equal, the focus was not on individuals, but on relationships, relationships between people and between ideas for the constant furthering of knowledge.

Although I did not choose to rely on feminist theory for this research, this idea of feminization merits investigation. I am left wondering how the comparatively large number of women and the focus on relationship contributed to my Inkshed conversion.

In addition to this female presence at Inkshed, as in my positive Mormon experiences, I recognize a respected patriarchal figure. I have often found myself referring to Russ Hunt as "the father of inkshedding," and I realize now that in my head (but perhaps the community has done this too) I have assigned him the role of patriarch. English professor, American transplant, gray beard and graying hair—he is so much like my own English professor father, I wonder if I have not, in some way, assumed the same role—respectful, unquestioning, eager for approval. The questions that arise from these self-reflections lead me back to the other side of the Inkshed border. Am I so obedient to the rules of inkshedding and Inkshed because of Russ? Do my philosophies of teaching writing come from my own process of arriving at them, or are they so closely aligned with Russ's because of my perceptions of Russ? Is my successful participation in Inkshed a result of trying to please the father figure, or an impression that somehow I have?

These surprising ways that my research has impacted identity and membership in my life have left me with different perspectives than I anticipated as well as many questions to explore. As I explained earlier, identity is a process, and that process incorporates a myriad of influences. Sometimes, depending on the context, one part of the process may be more dominant than another such as the role of academic in a university classroom. On the other hand, however, borders cross because my identity is complex, and although I continue to believe that I am at once a mother, a teacher, a student, a girlfriend, an Inkshedder, I cannot help but wonder if this concept of identity (like the criticisms leveled against Wenger's use of the term "community" for its utopian connotations (Cox, 2005)) is not too altruistic, simplistic, and dismissive of the reality of the intricacy of individual identity. I am sensitive to this because my Inkshed and Mormon identities seem negatively reciprocally intertwined. That is, as my Inkshed identity has grown and solidified, and I have moved into a position of full participation, my practices in the Mormon community have decreased. Although I can no more cease to be a Mormon than I can a Horne since it is part of my cultural heritage, I no longer claim a Mormon identity. When forced to, I admit to being a "bad Mormon." For some reason, these two identities, Mormon and Inkshedder, seem unable to co-exist—I cannot fully participate in both communities. Thus, in this case, identity is not only about a process of membership, but also a process of disfellowship.

Implications

With these lessons now articulated and packaged, a book ready to be sent to the publisher, and everything checked off my list, how is this research going to carry forward? What are the implications? Two things come to mind: pedagogy and belief.

Pedagogy

First and most importantly, this has an impact on how I approach teaching. The feelings of students whom I described in my opening vignette resonate with me in real and powerful ways and I try to stay open to and acknowledge those feelings. I try to make the writing that I do with my students dialogic. I try to give them opportunities for authentic, meaningful interactions through writing. When giving an assignment, I struggle between the demands of institutional requirements and the things I have learned at Inkshed about writing assignments. Theories of writing and composition jump to the forefront of my teaching. I try to help students link specific forms with recurring rhetorical contexts. I try to help them use writing as discovery and as a way of learning. Through my participation in Inkshed, I have learned that writing pedagogy is not only form, not only process, and not only social context, but an effort to help students understand all these aspects of their written communication.

As a direct result of my inkshedding experiences I also use writing specifically for community building. I have come to believe that writing well in a community leads to confidence. Understanding a community of peers and having that community support your writing leads to self assurance, improved writing, and increased skills and strategies in writing such as the ability to understand rhetorical context.

My awareness of students like Abby, whom I described at the beginning of this chapter, has been heightened. When I hear colleagues complaining that their students "can't write" or students themselves saying "I can't write; I'm not a writer" (as they often do when handing in assignments), I cringe. Writing is not simply knowing where to put commas or how to make subjects and verbs agree. Writing is about being a member of an academic community. Denying a student's ability to write denies them that membership. They need to be given tools to belong.

Belief

Second, there is, sometimes, as I have described earlier, a passion and enthusiasm in academia for the things we practice, teach, and research that resonates with religious concepts of belief, faith, and even zealotry in the way we want to proclaim the "truth." Understanding religious-type practices of academia helps to lay bare the spiritual nature of academia.

My experiences in the Inkshed community forced me to move away from the sterile and convenient explanation of spirituality afforded by my religious background. I turned instead to a broader conceptualization of spirituality that understands spirituality to be transcendent. Salman Rushdie (1990) defined this best when he wrote: "What I mean by transcendence is that flight of the human spirit outside the confines of its material, physical existence which all of us, secular or religious, experience on at least a few occasions"

(p. 103). This sense of transcendence made me feel unified in pursuit of a greater good with those around me and it was a delivery from the narrow confines of my self-absorbed insecurities.

I would suggest that this sense of transcendence, in fact, underscores much of the drive in academic life—the idealistic pursuit of something greater. Inkshedding, for example, illustrates the spiritual zeal that motivates much of writing studies—a strong belief in the things being taught and practiced, a belief in something more encompassing than an individual classroom or assignment, and adherence to ritual regular practices to reinforce the common beliefs. What scholar was not drawn to academia out of a passion for something he or she believed in, for something that promised to be bigger and more beneficial to which he or she could contribute? What successful scholar does not engage in the practices of academia that reinforce the values and beliefs of the field? Was the institution itself not founded on a quest for higher knowledge and higher learning for the betterment of humankind?

Language of belief, passion, faith, self, and emotions come up against current traditions of positivism, objectivity, and intellectual rigour that typically describe the academy. As a result, we may fail to see the connections between secular pursuits and spiritual pursuits. However, my experiences suggest that this connection is worth exploring as a way of tapping into and invigorating academic studies.

A favorite quote of mine comes from Alexander Pope who is credited with saying, "A little learning is a dangerous thing; drink deep, or taste not the Pierian spring." Community membership is not without costs whether through the price of practice or the sacrificing of an identity. Without the price, however, there is no opportunity to belong. Belonging promises identity. A little inkshedding, a little writing, is never enough. Membership comes from much writing, much deep drinking.

References

Artemeva, N. (2006). A time to speak, a time to act: A rhetorical genre analysis of a novice engineer's calculated risk taking. In N. Artemeva & A. Freedman (Eds.), *Rhetorical genre studies and beyond* (pp. 190-237). Winnipeg, MB: Inkshed Publications.

Artemeva, N., & Freedman, A. (Eds.). (2006). *Rhetorical genre studies and beyond*. Winnipeg, MB: Inkshed Publications.

Bakhtin, M. (1986). The problem of speech genres. In C. Emerson & M. Holquist (Eds.), *Bakhtin: Speech genres and other late essays*. Trans. V. McGee (pp. 60-102). Austin, TX: University of Texas Press.

Barton, D. (2000). Researching literacy practices: Learning from activities with teachers and students. In D. Barton, M. Hamilton, & R. Ivanič (Eds.), *Situated literacies: Reading and writing in context* (pp. 165-174). London: Routledge.

Barton, D., & Hamilton, M. (2005). Literacy, reification and the dynamics of social interaction. In D. Barton & K. Tusting (Eds.),

Beyond communities of practice: Language, power and social context (pp. 14-35). New York: Cambridge University Press.

Barton, D., & Tusting, K. (2005). Introduction. In D. Barton & K. Tusting (Eds.), *Beyond communities of practice: Language, power and social context* (pp. 1-13). New York: Cambridge University Press.

Bazerman, C. (1994). Systems of genres and the enactment of social intentions. In A. Freedman & P. Medway (Eds.), *Genre and the new rhetoric* (pp. 79-101). Bristol, PA: Taylor & Francis.

Bazerman, C. (2004). Speech acts, genres, and activity systems: How texts organize activity and people. In C. Bazerman & P. Prior (Eds.), *What writing does and how it does it: An introduction to analyzing texts and textual practices* (pp. 309-339). Mahwah, NJ: Lawrence Erlbaum.

Berkenkotter, C., & Huckin, T. (1995). *Genre knowledge in disciplinary communication: Cognition/culture/power.* Hillsdale, NJ: Lawrence Erlbaum.

Berlin, J. (1988). Rhetoric and ideology in the writing class. *College English, 50*(5), 477-494. Retrieved from http://www.jstor.org/stable/377477

Bizzell, P. (1983). Cognition, convention, and certainty: What we need to know about writing. *PRE/TEXT, 3,* 213-243.

Bourdieu, P. (1977). *Outline of a theory of practice.* Cambridge, UK: Cambridge University Press.

Bruffee, K. A. (1986). Social construction, language, and the authority of knowledge: A bibliographic essay. *College English, 48*(8), 773-790. Retrieved from http://www.jstor.org/stable/376723

Bruner, J. (1990). *Acts of meaning.* Cambridge, MA: Harvard University Press.

Bullock, C. (1982, December). News from the provinces: Alberta. *W&R/T&P Newsletter, 1*(3), 5-6.

Burke, K. (1941). *The philosophy of literary form.* Berkeley: University of California Press.

Clandinin, D., & Connelly, F. (2000). *Narrative inquiry: Experience and story in qualitative research.* San Francisco, CA: Jossey-Bass.

Coe, R. M. (1983, March). News from the provinces: British Columbia. *W&R/T&P Newsletter, 2*(2), 2-4.

Coffey, A., & Atkinson, P. (1996). *Making sense of qualitative data: Complementary research strategies.* Thousand Oaks, CA: Sage.

Cox, A. (2005). What are communities of practice? A comparative review of four seminal works. *Journal of Information Science, 31*(6), 527-540. Retrieved from http://jis.sagepub.com/cgi/content/refs/31/6/527

Creese, A. (2005). Mediating allegations of racism in a multiethnic London school: What speech communities and communities of practice tell us about discourse and power. In D. Barton & K. Tusting (Eds.), *Beyond communities of practice: Language, power and social context* (pp. 55-76). New York: Cambridge University Press.

Davies, A. (1996). *Team teaching relationships: Teachers' stories and stories of school on the professional knowledge landscape.* Unpublished doctoral dissertation, University of Alberta.

Devitt, A. (2004). *Writing genres.* Carbondale: Southern Illinois University Press.

Dias, P., Freedman, A., Medway, P., & Paré, A. (1999). *Worlds apart: Acting and writing in academic and workplace contexts.* Mahwah, NJ: Lawrence Erlbaum.

Drain, S. (1984, September). Thanks—and a testimonial. *Inkshed 3*(4), 2.

Elbow, P. (1973). *Writing without teachers.* New York: Oxford University Press.

Ellis, C., & Bochner, A. (2000). Autoethnography, personal narrative, reflexivity: Researcher as subject. In N. K. Denzin & Y. S. Lincoln (Eds.), *Handbook of qualitative research* (2nd ed., pp. 733-768). Thousand Oaks, CA: Sage.

Emig, J. (1971). *The composing processes of twelfth graders. Research report No. 13.* Urbana, IL: National Council of Teachers of English.

Faigley, L. (1986). Competing theories of process: A critique and a proposal. *College English, 48*(6), 527-542. Retrieved from http://www.jstor.org/stable/376707

Flower, L., & Hayes, J. R. (1981). A cognitive process theory of writing. *College Composition and Communication, 32*(4), 365-387. Retrieved from http://www.jstor.org/stable/356600

Freadman, A. (1994). Anyone for tennis? In A. Freedman & P. Medway (Eds.), *Genre and the new rhetoric* (pp. 43-66). Bristol, PA: Taylor & Francis.

Freedman, A., & Medway, P. (1994). Locating genre studies: Antecedents and prospects. In A. Freedman & P. Medway (Eds.), *Genre and the new rhetoric* (pp. 1-20). Bristol, PA: Taylor & Francis.

Geertz, C. (1973). *The interpretation of cultures*. New York: Basic Books.

Giroux, H., & McLaren, P. (1994). *Between borders: Pedagogy and the politics of cultural studies.* New York: Routledge.

Glaser, B., & Strauss, A. (1967). *The discovery of grounded theory: Strategies for qualitative research.* Chicago: Aldine.

Graves, H., Hyland, T., & Graves, R. (2006, Fall). Inkshed 24 call for papers. *Inkshed, 23*(2-3), 17-18. Retrieved from http://www.inkshed.ca/nlettc06/23.2.pdf

Handley, K., Sturdy, A., Fincham, R., & Clark, T. (2006). Within and beyond communities of practice: Making sense of learning through participation, identity and practice. *Journal of Management Studies, 43*(3), 641-653. Retrieved from http://onlinelibrary.wiley. com/doi/10.1111/j.1467-6486.2006.00605.x/abstract

Hine, C. (2000). *Virtual ethnography*. London: Sage.

Horne, M. (2004, Spring). Learning to inkshed: Learning to belong. *Inkshed, 21*(1). Retrieved from http://www.stthomasu.ca/inkshed/ nlett604/horne.htm

Horne, M. (2008). Community membership through socially situated writing processes: A journey of inkshedding into Inkshed. Unpublished doctoral dissertation, McGill University, Montreal, QC.

Hunt, R. (2004). *What is inkshedding?* Retrieved from http://www. stthomasu.ca/~hunt/dialogic/whatshed.htm

Inkshed 23. (2006, May 5). [Edited inksheds—Session #1]. Retrieved from http://www.stthomasu.ca/inkshed/inkshed23/ edsheds/miriam.htm

Inkshed 2000 Live Archive. (2000, May 11). Inkshedding selections— Session 5. Retrieved from http://www.stthomasu.ca/inkshed/ shed2000edsheds5.htm

Kuhn, T. (1970). *The structure of scientific revolutions*. Chicago: University of Chicago Press.

Lankshear, C., Gee, J., Knobel, M., & Searle, C. (1997). *Changing literacies*. Buckingham, UK: Open University Press.

Lave, J., & Wenger, E. (1991). *Situated learning: Legitimate peripheral participation*. Cambridge, UK: Cambridge University Press.

LeFevre, K. B. (1987). *Invention as a social act*. Carbondale: Southern Illinois University Press.

Lincoln, Y. S., & Guba, E. G. (1985). *Naturalistic inquiry*. Thousand Oaks, CA: Sage.

Maykut, P., & Morehouse, R. (1994). *Beginning qualitative research: A philosophic and practical guide.* London: Falmer.

Medway, P. (2002). Fuzzy genres and community identities: The case of architecture students' sketchbooks. In R. Coe, L. Lingard, & T. Teslenko (Eds.), *The rhetoric and ideology of genre* (pp. 123-153). Cresskill, NJ: Hampton.

Miller, C. (1984). Genre as social action. *Quarterly Journal of Speech, 70*(2), 151-167. Retrieved from http://www.mendeley.com/research/genre-as-social-action/

Murray, D. M. (1969). Finding your own voice: Teaching composition in an age of dissent. *College Composition and Communication, 20*(2), 118-123. Retrieved from http://tinyurl.com/83l8vkb

Paré, A. (2002). Genre and identity: Individuals, institutions, and ideology. In R. Coe, L. Lingard, & T. Teslenko (Eds.), *The rhetoric and ideology of genre* (pp. 57-72). Cresskill, NJ: Hampton.

Paré, A., & Smart, G. (1994). Observing genres in action: Towards a research methodology. In A. Freedman & P. Medway (Eds.), *Genre and the new rhetoric* (pp. 146-154). Bristol, PA: Taylor & Francis.

Patton, M. (1982). *Practical evaluation.* Thousand Oaks, CA: Sage.

Patton, M. (2002). *Qualitative research and evaluation methods.* Thousand Oaks, CA: Sage.

Reither, J. (1982a, October). *A newsletter for educators in Canada interested in writing and reading/theory and practice. 1*(1), 1.

Reither, J. (1982b, November). Consultants. *W&R/T&P Newsletter, 1*(2), 7.

Reither, J. (1983, September). One year of W&R/T&P. *W&R/T&P Newsletter, 2*(5), 1-2.

Rogoff, B., & Lave, J. (Eds.). (1984). *Everyday cognition: Its development in social context.* Cambridge, MA: Harvard University Press.

Rorty, R. (1979). *Philosophy and the mirror of nature*. Princeton, NJ: Princeton University Press.

Rushdie, S. (1990). Is nothing sacred? *Granta, 31*(Spring), 97-111.

Seidman, I. (1991). *Interviewing as qualitative research*. New York: Teachers College Press.

Schryer, C. (1994). The lab vs. the clinic: Sites of competing genres. In A. Freedman & P. Medway (Eds.), *Genre and the new rhetoric* (pp. 105-124). Bristol, PA: Taylor & Francis.

Smith, T. (2000). Inkshed—"What kind of shed are you?" A micro-ethnography of the CASLL/ Inkshed listserv and conference Inkshed Website, *Canadian Association for the Study of Language and Learning*. Retrieved from http://www.stthomasu.ca/inkshed/shed2000/tsethnog.htm

Strauss, A. (1987). *Qualitative research for social scientists*. New York: Cambridge University Press.

Street, B. (1985). *Literacy in theory and practice*. New York: Cambridge University Press.

Tajfel, H., & Turner, J. C. (1986). An integrative theory of intergroup conflict. In S. Worchel & W. Austin (Eds.), *Psychology of intergroup relations* (pp. 2-24). Chicago: Nelson-Hall.

Taylor, C. (1994). The politics of recognition. In A. Gutmann (Ed.), *Multiculturalism: Examining the politics of recognition* (pp. 25-74). New York: Princeton University Press.

Tusting, K. (2005). Language and power in communities of practice. In D. Barton & K. Tusting (Eds.), *Beyond communities of practice: Language, power and social context* (pp. 36-54). New York: Cambridge University Press.

Van Manen, M. (1997). *Researching lived experience: Human science for an action sensitive pedagogy* (2nd ed.). London, ON: Althouse.

Wenger, E. (1998). *Communities of practice: Learning, meaning, and identity.* New York: Cambridge University Press.

Wenger, E. (2006, June). *Communities of practice: A brief introduction.* Retrieved from http://www.ewenger.com/theory

West, C. (1993). *Race matters.* Boston, MA: Beacon Press.

Appendices

Appendix A Inkshed Timeline

1979—Aviva Freedman and Ian Pringle organize the first international conference devoted entirely to writing in Canada, at Carleton University, Ottawa.

1982 (summer)—Jim Reither, Russ Hunt, Chris Bullock, Anne Greenwood, David Reiter, Susan Stevenson, and Kay Stewart meet at a conference in Wyoming and spend time discussing the need for a Canadian forum for discussions of writing studies.

1982 (September)—Jim Reither and Russ Hunt print the inaugural issue of a newsletter for those interested in teaching and learning in reading and writing.

1982 (November)—Russ Hunt and Jim Reither begin the W&R/T&P (Writing and Reading/Theory and Practice) newsletter out of St. Thomas University in Fredericton, New Brunswick.

1983 (December)—The newsletter takes on the official title of "Inkshed."

1984—The first Inkshed conference is held in Fredericton, New Brunswick.

1985—At the second Inkshed conference in Edmonton, Alberta, talent night is included; the conference is confirmed as an annual event.

1992—A Constitution is passed at the Annual General Meeting signaling the official formation of The Canadian Association for the Study of Language and Learning (CASLL).

1995—The CASLL listserv begins.

Appendix B Inkshed Conferences

1984—Inkshed I Fredericton, New Brunswick

1985—Inkshed II Edmonton, Alberta

1986—Inkshed III Montreal, Quebec

1987—Inkshed IV Winnipeg, Manitoba

1988—Inkshed V St. John's, Newfoundland

1989—Inkshed VI Bowen Island, British Columbia

1990—Inkshed VII Halifax, Nova Scotia

1991—Inkshed VIII Saint-Marc-sur-Richelieu, Quebec

1992—Inkshed IX Banff, Alberta

1993—Inkshed X The Opinicon, Portland, Ontario

1994—Inkshed XI Fredericton, New Brunswick

1995—Inkshed XII Kananaskis, Alberta

1996—Inkshed XIII Hecla Island, Manitoba

1997—Inkshed XIV Lake Couchiching, Orillia, Ontario

1998—Inkshed XV Oak Island, Nova Scotia

1999—Inkshed XVI Mont Gabriel, Quebec

2000—Inkshed XVII Bowen Island, British Columbia

2001—Inkshed XVIII Canmore, Alberta

2002—Inkshed XIX Stanhope by the Sea, Prince Edward Island

2003—Inkshed XX Hockley Highlands, Orangeville, Ontario

2004—Inkshed XXI Sun Peaks, Kamloops, British Columbia

2005—Inkshed XXII White Point, Nova Scotia

2006—Inkshed XXIII Gimli, Manitoba

2007—Inkshed XXIV London, Ontario

2008—Inkshed XXV Fredericton, New Brunswick

2009—[not numbered] Ottawa, Ontario [meeting after CASDW]

2010—Inkshed XXVI Montreal, Quebec
      [one-day conference with an AGM]

2011—Inkshed XXVII Fredericton, New Brunswick
      [one-day conference with an AGM]

2012—Inkshed XXVIII Toronto, Ontario

Appendix C Design

T he following is excerpted, with minor editing, from my doctoral dissertation (Horne, 2008) entitled *Community Membership through Socially Situated Writing Processes: A Journey of Inkshedding into Inkshed.*

Design

Before data collection about a community can begin, ethnographers and narrative inquirers must first gain access to the community. Because this study recounts my journey of membership into Inkshed, the entire study reflects the ways in which I gained access to the Inkshed community. Although I draw on experiences of other Inkshedders to confirm and validate the kinds of experiences I had, my conclusions are based on my own experiences and how they resonated with others. This journey, however, began with a few preliminary steps, which I describe here. These are followed by a description of data collection methods and analysis.

Access

My initial access to the community came through my contact with some of my committee members who have a long history with the Inkshed community. When I first began to conceive this study, I understood inkshedding as a classroom activity. Doctoral committee members Ann Beer and Anthony Paré have both participated in Inkshed conferences for many years, and they helped me understand that there is an entire community and culture behind the activity. They are well-respected members of the community and I used my association with them to begin to make contacts with other community members—primarily, Russ Hunt. At their suggestion, I entered into email correspondence with Russ. In this way, by the time I attended my first conference, I already had established relationships with community members who were aware of my intentions to study inkshedding and Inkshed.

When I attended my first conference, I did so with an open agenda. In other words, I made it clear from my first introductions to community members that my intentions were to study inkshedding and Inkshed. There was, I believe, some initial suspicion of my motives. One woman, on hearing of my intentions, asked if I was there to spy on them. Her comments sprang from the work of a graduate student a few years earlier who came to the conference and listened in on people's conversations, then asked if she could quote them. I tried from the outset to be transparent about my motives and to show that my process was an emergent one—that I was not trying to prove anything about inkshedding.

One challenge to my access was not the community, but instead, my own inhibitions and shyness. It was difficult for me to talk to people—and despite Anthony's assurances that everyone would be friendly (which they were), I was unsure of and uncomfortable in myself and unclear as to how to proceed. I will explain how I set about gathering data to explore my questions.

Data Collection, Methods and Procedures

Data collection took a variety of forms and drew from several methodologies—phenomenology, ethnography, autoethnography, and narrative inquiry. For the purposes of organization, the terminology for the kinds of data collection I describe come from Clandinin and Connelly (2000). The actual practices overlapped throughout the qualitative methods that I drew from.

i. Autobiographical Writing

As Clandinin and Connelly explained, "autobiographical writing is a way to write about the whole context of a life" (p. 101). Early on in my research, as I found myself being drawn into the community, I felt the need to understand my position, that is, my role as a researcher of Inkshed juxtaposed to the rest of my life. As a result, I spent many months reflecting on my position in Inkshed as a participant and as a researcher, as well as my personal writing position. I examined the ways in which my outside life experiences impacted the experiences that I was having in the Inkshed community and inkshedding activity. I did this through multiple autobiographical explorations, pieces of which are included throughout this book in the form of vignettes.

ii. Journal Writing

Journal writing proved to be important in this study. At conferences and in between, I spent a great deal of time writing in a journal and describing not just the things that I was seeing and doing, but my reaction and feelings about these things (Lincoln & Guba, 1985). While not every detail recorded in my journals became a significant piece of data in this research, the small details together helped me to begin to see patterns and themes. As Clandinin and Connelly (2000) explained: "What may have appeared to be insignificant nothingness at the time they were composed as field texts may take on a pattern as they are interwoven with other field texts in the construction of research texts" (p. 104). Indeed, as I brought the experiences I recorded in my journal into the other data I was looking at, I found that my recorded thoughts facilitated comprehension of the things I was trying to understand.

iii. Field Notes

As I attended conferences, I took extensive field notes; I almost always had a pad of paper with me. This was, in fact, unobtrusive when I was in the conference room as many people at the conference take copious notes throughout presentations, or jot down thoughts as they come to them. At events such as the talent show, walks in the wood, or evening socializing at the bar when it seemed intrusive to carry a notebook, I made mental observations and recorded them in writing as soon as I could. I tried, as much as possible, to record the things that I saw and to be aware of how my interpretations influenced my notes (Maykut & Morehouse, 1994). My notes included diagrams of the set-up of the rooms, lists of speakers and themes, reactions of participants, accounts of spontaneous discussions, and jokes. These notes were a constant reminder to me that I was working as a researcher. At times, when I found myself caught up in the conference as a participant—through the presentations, inkshedding, discussions, or other activities—I would forget my role as researcher and fail to take notes. While this may have led to less comprehensive field notes, I believe that it led me to be able to explore a different aspect of the conference. The other data that I compiled helped to flesh out the kinds of things I was seeing in my notes.

iv. Letters

The Inkshed community is spread far and wide and members meet only once a year as a large group. Even then, not every Inkshedder goes to every conference. Therefore, a useful source of data collection for me was letters, all sent and received via email. I used virtual ethnography, a form of ethnography that uses technology to mediate interactions and challenges notions of face-to-face interactions (Hine, 2000). I frequently used email to communicate with Inkshedders in order to get answers to questions—much like an interview. The advantage to working in written text rather than a face-to-face interview is that the respondents had time to ponder the questions before responding. As Davies (1996) explained:

> The thing about letters is the fact that you can get in
> touch with your own thoughts and feelings, in your own
> time and space. It allows, I believe, for a deeper level
> of reflection on the part of the writers. (p. 176)

For example, some of my participants took weeks to respond to my queries and when they did, they would answer with pages and pages of carefully thought out detail. Others responded quickly and sometimes followed up with second and third responses as more ideas came to them. Inkshedders are writers and communicators. Therefore, this was a rich source of data for me.

v. Conversation

Inkshed conferences are designed to promote discussion. The writing activity is a way of facilitating discussion so that ideas are constantly being reinserted into the ongoing dialogues. Meals, coffee breaks, entertainment, housing—all of these things happen together so that participants have as much opportunity as possible to engage in dialogic communication. Thus, I was able to engage in many casual conversations about Inkshed and inkshedding. Many people who knew that I was studying inkshedding approached me in a casual setting to be able to share their experiences with me without the pressure of a formal interview complete with tape recorder. These conversations helped me to get a feeling for the kinds of experiences that other people were having but often did not feel comfortable sharing with the group at large.

In addition to face-to-face conversations, Inkshed hosts a listserv, which encourages on-line discussions. The advantage to this is that people from across Canada can participate in a conversation, and they have time to sort out their thoughts before jumping in. I occasionally started discussions this way, but most often lurked and listened in to hear what issues were most important, or what kinds of topics came up in discussions.

vi. Interviews

Following the work of Maykut and Morehouse (1994), Patton (1982), and Seidman (1991), I designed semi-structured, open-ended interviews. These interviews took place with members of the Inkshed community. I conducted interviews with both individuals and groups. Although I had general categories of questions that I hoped they would answer, I allowed the interviews to go on tangents and explored different areas as they arose. I felt that it was important to hear what these participants thought was important to say because, as Patton (1982) explained, the purpose of an interview "is not to put things in someone's mind, but rather, to access the perspective of the person being interviewed. We interview people to find out from them those things that we cannot directly observe" (p. 161).

Patton further expounded on the usefulness of interviewing by explaining that, as human instruments, it is impossible for researchers to observe everything. Thus, by asking questions, new information becomes available; new perspectives emerge. I explored these perspectives by taking notes during interviews, recording and transcribing the interviews, and then carefully studying the transcriptions.

vii. Documents

Documents from the Inkshed community provided a rich resource for learning more about the community, its culture, its values and the way it functions. Included in the documents were historical texts, including access to all of the *Inkshed* newsletters, the archive for the listserv, and the CASLL constitution. These documents helped to shape my understanding of how the community has grown and changed over the years. They also helped to explain fundamental values of the community.

In addition to the historical documents, I was able to use documents produced at the conferences I attended. One of these was "The Wall." This was the result of a twenty-year retrospective done at the Inkshed XX conference in 2003 by Nan Johnson and Sharron Wall. They lined the conference room with posters and asked everyone in attendance to contribute by writing their seminal Inkshed moments on post-it notes and sticking them to the posters. They included experiences, influential readings, and even talent show memories. I was able to use this document to get a sense of the community and the things that had shaped it. Often, small details emerged in "The Wall" that did not emerge elsewhere, yet contributed in important ways to my study.

As well as "The Wall," I was able to use inkshedding texts. At two conferences, I presented parts of my research and participants responded through their inkshedding. I was able to use these texts to verify the things I was seeing in my research as well as to refocus and generate new lines of questioning.

This broad variety of field texts provided multiple sources of data. By having such complex and multiple sets of data, I was able to compare different sets in order to see and study emergent themes.

Analysis

The analysis of my experiences through the data proved challenging. In this section, I describe the tools that I used to make sense of the data. The categories of analysis are evident through the subheadings that I use throughout various chapters to describe different aspects of my Inkshed and inkshedding experiences.

i. Writing

My primary means of analyzing my data was to write about it. Advocates of process writing (Elbow, 1973; Emig, 1971; Faigley, 1986; Flower & Hayes, 1981; Murray, 1969) understood that through writing, ideas, knowledge, and learning emerged. Van Manen (1997) argued the importance of writing in data analysis because it forces the researcher to at once reflect and introspect but still consider the world. Thus, it has been through the writing of interim texts (Clandinin & Connelly, 2000) that I have struggled to make sense of my data. As the name implies, interim texts are "texts situated in the spaces between field texts and final, published research texts" (p. 133). These texts provide a place to try out ideas. They are full of false starts, dead ends, emerging questions, and a struggle to make sense of and test out emergent themes and ideas. Often, I used these texts as a way of communicating to my supervisor where I was in my thinking. I would spend time writing, he would read, we would talk, and I would go back to write some more. Through these texts, I eventually came to the fundamental themes that I present in this document.

ii. Living with the Data

As I struggled to make sense of my data and understand what to do with it, the methodologist on my committee told me I needed to live with the data. I needed to immerse myself in it and hear what it was telling me. "Listen to the voices," he said. This meant reading, rereading, and rereading again without any preconceived interpretations. Much of this reading at the early stages was punctuated by interim writing that worked to make sense of what the data were telling me. Then I returned to the data again, reading and listening. As I did so, general themes and patterns began to emerge.

iii. Coding and Questioning

Once clear themes began to emerge, I began to organize my data according to the patterns I saw. From here, I was able to ask additional questions to further deepen my understandings of what I was looking at. To facilitate this questioning, I used the constant comparative method (Glaser & Strauss, 1967; Lincoln & Guba, 1985; Maykut & Morehouse, 1994), which is based on inductive analysis. I began by organizing and then categorizing my data based on common themes. I frequently refined my categories as I explored the data. I then looked at relationships across my different categories and used these relationships to integrate data from multiple sources.

In addition to the constant comparative method, I also followed Strauss's (1987) analytical approach that asks researchers to continually question the data in order to develop lines of hypothesis. Asking about the consequences of the themes that I saw emerging in the data led me to examine the data in diverse ways. These ideas were complemented by Coffey and Atkinson's (1996) analysis scheme that helped me look for patterns and themes as well as contrasts and paradoxes.

Another form of analysis that proved useful was a narrative analysis that looked at forms and functions. Much of the data I collected contained stories and anecdotes. As Coffey and Atkinson (1996) explained, "individual narratives are situated within particular interactions and within specific social, cultural, and institutional discourses" (p. 62). Therefore, I was able to look at the forms and functions that emerged into themes through the narratives in the data. Throughout all of this coding and questioning, I continued to write—testing out my findings, attempting to explain them, taking up new perspectives on them.